HBR's 10 Must Reads

UPDATED & EXPANDED

Mental Toughness

HBR's 10 Must Reads

HBR's 10 Must Reads are definitive collections of classic ideas, practical advice, and essential thinking from the pages of *Harvard Business Review*. Exploring topics like disruptive innovation, emotional intelligence, and new technology in our ever-evolving world, these books empower any leader to make bold decisions and inspire others.

TITLES INCLUDE:

    HBR's 10 Must Reads for New Managers
    HBR's 10 Must Reads on AI
    HBR's 10 Must Reads on Building a Great Culture
    HBR's 10 Must Reads on Change Management
    HBR's 10 Must Reads on Communication
    HBR's 10 Must Reads on Data Strategy
    HBR's 10 Must Reads on Decision-Making
    HBR's 10 Must Reads on Design Thinking
    HBR's 10 Must Reads on Digital Transformation
    HBR's 10 Must Reads on Emotional Intelligence
    HBR's 10 Must Reads on High Performance
    HBR's 10 Must Reads on Innovation
    HBR's 10 Must Reads on Leadership
    HBR's 10 Must Reads on Leading Winning Teams
    HBR's 10 Must Reads on Managing People
    HBR's 10 Must Reads on Managing Yourself
    HBR's 10 Must Reads on Marketing
    HBR's 10 Must Reads on Mental Toughness
    HBR's 10 Must Reads on Strategy
    HBR's 10 Must Reads on Women and Leadership
    HBR's 10 Must Reads Boxed Set (6 Books)
    HBR's 10 Must Reads Ultimate Boxed Set (14 Books)

For a full list, visit hbr.org/mustreads.

UPDATED & EXPANDED

Mental Toughness

Harvard Business Review Press
Boston, Massachusetts

HBR Press Quantity Sales Discounts

Harvard Business Review Press titles are available at significant quantity discounts when purchased in bulk for leadership development programs, client gifts, or sales promotions. Opportunities to co-brand copies with your logo or messaging are also available. For details and discount information for both print and ebook formats, contact booksales@hbr.org or visit www.hbr.org/bulksales.

Copyright 2025 Harvard Business School Publishing Corporation

All rights reserved

Printed in the United States of America

10 9 8 7 6 5 4 3 2 1

No part of this publication may be reproduced, stored in or introduced into a retrieval system, or transmitted, in any form, or by any means (electronic, mechanical, photocopying, recording, or otherwise), without the prior permission of the publisher. Requests for permission should be directed to permissions@harvardbusiness.org, or mailed to Permissions, Harvard Business School Publishing, 60 Harvard Way, Boston, Massachusetts 02163.

The web addresses referenced in this book were live and correct at the time of the book's publication but may be subject to change.

Library of Congress Cataloging-in-Publication data is forthcoming.

ISBN: 979-8-89279-191-5
eISBN: 979-8089279-192-2

The paper used in this publication meets the requirements of the American National Standard for Permanence of Paper for Publications and Documents in Libraries and Archives Z39.48-1992.

Contents

1 How to Bounce Back from Adversity   1
A method to understand—and redirect—your instinctive reaction to crises.

by Joshua D. Margolis and Paul G. Stoltz

2 How to Overcome Your Fear of the Unknown   17
Embrace the transformative potential of uncertainty.

by Nathan Furr and Susannah Harmon Furr

> QUICK READ

How to Stop Worrying About What Other People Think of You   29
Fear of other people's opinions is getting in the way of your own values.

by Michael Gervais

3 Give Yourself a Break: The Power of Self-Compassion   35
When you have a setback, treat yourself as you would a friend.

by Serena Chen

> **QUICK READ**

How to Stop Dwelling on Your Stress   45
Four behavioral-science-backed techniques to help change your thinking.

by Jenny Taitz

4 Building Resilience   51
What business can learn from a pioneering army program for fostering post-traumatic growth.

by Martin E.P. Seligman

> **QUICK READ**

Do You Know When to Quit?   65
Research shows the benefits and downsides of perseverance.

by André Spicer

5 Beating Burnout   71
How to tell if you have it and what to do about it.

by Monique Valcour

> **QUICK READ**

Burnout Is About Your Workplace, Not Your People   83
Leaders create the conditions that lead to burnout—or prevent it.

by Jennifer Moss

6 An Antidote to Incivility 91
How to protect yourself from rude colleagues.

by Christine Porath

QUICK READ

Recognizing and Responding to Microaggressions at Work 101
What to do when you notice a colleague—or yourself—saying something harmful.

by Ella F. Washington

7 Handling Fierce Criticism and Personal Attacks 113
How to steel yourself, pause, and think on your feet.

An interview with Ruchika T. Malhotra and Patti Neuhold-Ravikumar by Amy Bernstein

8 The Making of a Corporate Athlete 125
Recovering energy is as important as expending it.

by Jim Loehr and Tony Schwartz

9 Why Career Transition Is So Hard 147
And how to manage it better.

by Herminia Ibarra

10 Organizational Grit 159
How to turn passion and perseverance into performance.

by Thomas H. Lee and Angela L. Duckworth

Discussion Guide	177
Notes	181
About the Contributors	183
Index	187

UPDATED & EXPANDED

Mental Toughness

How to Bounce Back from Adversity

by Joshua D. Margolis and Paul G. Stoltz

Things are humming along, and then: A top client calls and says, "We're switching suppliers, starting next month. I'm afraid your company no longer figures into our plans." Or three colleagues, all of whom joined the organization around the same time you did, are up for promotion—but you aren't. Or your team loses another good person in a third round of layoffs; weak markets or no, you still need to make your numbers, but now you'll have to rely heavily on two of the most uncooperative members of the group.

So how do you react? Are you angry and disappointed, ranting and raving to anyone who will listen? Do you feel dejected and victimized, resigned to the situation even as you deny the cold reality of it? Or do you experience a rush of excitement—perhaps tinged with fear—because you sense an opportunity to develop your skills and talents in ways you'd never imagined? The truth is, you've probably reacted in all those ways when confronted with a challenge—maybe even cycling through multiple emotional states in the course of dealing with one really big mess.

Whatever your initial reaction, however, the challenge is to turn a negative experience into a productive one—that is, to counter adversity with resilience. Psychological resilience is the capacity to respond quickly and constructively to crises. It's a central dynamic in most survival stories, such as those of the shell-shocked individuals and organizations that rallied in the wake of 9/11 and Hurricane Katrina. But resilience can be hard to muster for many reasons: Fear, anger, and confusion can paralyze us after a severe setback. Assigning blame rather than generating solutions is an all-too-human tendency. Worse yet, those to whom we turn for counsel may offer us exactly the wrong kind of advice.

Decades of research in psychology, on topics including hardiness, learned helplessness, coping, and the correlation between cognitive style and health, confirms that each of us has a distinct, consistent pattern of thinking about life's twists and turns—a pattern of which most of us are largely unaware. It may be an unconscious reflex to look backward from traumatic incidents to explain what just happened. Such analysis can be useful, certainly—but only up to the point where strong negative emotions start to prevent our moving on.

We believe that managers can build high levels of resilience in themselves and their teams by taking charge of how they think about adversity. Resilient managers move quickly from analysis to a plan of action (and reaction). After the onset of adversity, they shift from cause-oriented thinking to response-oriented thinking, and their focus is strictly forward. In our work with leaders in a variety of companies and industries, we've identified four lenses through which managers can view adverse events to make this shift effectively.

Idea in Brief

The Problem

Psychological resilience—the capacity to respond quickly and constructively in a crisis—can be hard to muster when a manager is paralyzed by fear, anger, confusion, or a tendency to assign blame.

The Solution

Resilient managers shift quickly from endlessly dissecting traumatic events to looking forward, determining the best course of action given new realities. They understand the size and scope of the crisis and the levels of control and impact they may have in a bad situation.

The authors describe a resilience regiment—a series of pointed questions designed to help managers replace negative responses with creative, resourceful ones and to move forward despite real or perceived obstacles.

Control: When a crisis hits, do you look for what you can improve now rather than trying to identify all the factors—even those beyond your control—that caused it in the first place?

Impact: Can you sidestep the temptation to find the origins of the problem in yourself or others and focus instead on identifying what positive effects your personal actions might have?

Breadth: Do you assume that the underlying cause of the crisis is specific and can be contained, or do you worry that it might cast a long shadow over all aspects of your life?

Duration: How long do you believe that the crisis and its repercussions will last?

The first two lenses characterize an individual's personal reaction to adversity, and the second two capture his or her

> ## The Research Behind the Resilience Regimen
>
> Two converging streams of research informed our work. The first examines how patterns of understanding the world shape people's responses to stressful situations. Albert Ellis and Aaron Beck pioneered this research, followed by, among others, Martin Seligman and Christopher Peterson on learned helplessness; Richard Lazarus and Susan Folkman on coping; and Lyn Abramson, David Burns, and James Amirkhan on how "attributional styles" affect health. More recently, Karen Reivich and Andrew Shatté identified how people can strengthen their resilience.
>
> The second stream, pioneered by Suzanne Ouellette and Salvatore Maddi in their studies of hardiness and extended most recently by Deborah Khoshaba and Aaron Antonovsky, explored what differentiated two groups of people who encountered intense stress. One group flourished while the other sank.
>
> A common finding emerges from these two streams of inquiry: How people approach trying circumstances influences both their ability to deal with them and, ultimately, their own success and well-being.

impressions of the adversity's magnitude. Managers should consider all four to fully understand their instinctive responses to personal and professional challenges, setbacks, or failures.

In the following pages we'll describe a deliberative rather than reflexive approach to dealing with hardship—what we call a *resilience regimen*. By asking a series of pointed questions, managers can grasp their own and their direct reports' habits of thought and help reframe negative events in productive ways. With the four lenses as a guide, they can learn to stop feeling paralyzed by crisis, respond with strength and creativity, and help their direct reports do the same.

When Adversity Strikes

Most of us go with our gut when something bad happens. Deeply ingrained habits and beliefs sap our energy and keep us from acting constructively. People commonly fall into one of two emotional traps. One is *deflation*. Someone who has marched steadily through a string of successes can easily come to feel like a hero, able to fix any problem single-handedly. A traumatic event can snap that person back to reality. Even for the less heroic among us, adversity can touch off intense bursts of negative emotion—as if a dark cloud had settled behind our eyes, as one manager described it. We may feel disappointed in ourselves or others, mistreated and dispirited, even besieged.

That was the case with an executive we'll call Andrea, who headed up a major subsidiary of a U.S. automotive parts supplier. She had put up with years of internal bickering and the company's calcified cost structure. But over time she managed to bring the warring factions—unions, management, engineers, and marketers—together, and she gained widespread approval for a plan that would phase out old facilities and reduce crippling costs: Rather than try to supply every make and manufacturer, the company would focus on the truck market. Even more important, Andrea rallied everyone around a new line of products and a clear value proposition for customers that would rejuvenate the company's brand. The future looked bright.

Then fuel prices skyrocketed, the economy seized up, and demand from all segments of the truck market evaporated almost overnight. The recession had brought unfathomable challenges to the organization, and their suddenness left Andrea feeling as if she'd been socked in the stomach. After all her hard work, difficult conversations, and strategizing to fix the previous problems, she felt overmatched—for the first time in her career. Andrea lacked resilience precisely because she had a long history of wins.

The other emotional trap is *victimization*. Many of us assume the role of helpless bystander in the face of an adverse event. "Those people" have put us in an unfortunate position, we tell ourselves (and others) again and again. We dismiss both criticism and helpful suggestions from others, and go out of our way to affirm that we're right, everyone else is wrong, and no one understands us. Meanwhile, self-doubt may creep in, making us feel hopelessly constrained by circumstances.

Greg, a senior business development manager at an electronic accessories company, felt just this way. He had sailed through his first three years at the company with several promotions, taking on increasing responsibility—first for building brand awareness among younger consumers, and then for building new relationships (and gaining more shelf space) with large retailers throughout the United States and Canada. But as global competition heated up, Greg's peers and superiors asked him to rethink his approach and questioned whether retail outlets were still a viable distribution channel. Big-box stores were squeezing the company's margins, and physically servicing all the company's accounts seemed unnecessarily expensive compared with online options. Greg reacted to his colleagues' requests by becoming more and more defensive and extremely angry.

These stories illustrate the two-headed hydra of contemporary adversity. First, highly accomplished managers are confronting, in rapid succession, challenges the likes of which they've never seen before—a worldwide economic crisis, the globalization of business, the rise of new technologies, deep demographic shifts. Feeling discouraged and helpless, they turn away from

> ## Coaching Resilience
>
> Often even the most resilient managers run into trouble trying to coach direct reports in crisis. They react with either a how-to pep talk delivered utterly without empathy or understanding, or a sympathetic ear and reassurance that things will turn out OK. Neither response will equip your team members to handle the next unforeseen twist or turn. Instead, you should adopt a collaborative, inquisitive approach that can help your direct reports generate their own options and possibilities.
>
> Suppose a defensive employee were self-aware enough to ask you, his mentor, for help dealing with a professional setback—say, being passed over for promotion. You could just acknowledge his feelings and basically manage his response for him—outlining who he needs to talk to and in what order, and what to do if he doesn't get the answers he wants. But if you ask specifying, visualizing, and collaborating questions—such as "How can you step up to make the most immediate, positive impact on this situation?" and "How do you think your efforts in that direction would affect your team and your peers?"—you put the ball back in your employee's court. You're not endorsing any particular perspective, you're not providing absolute answers—you're helping to build resilience in a team member.

the problem and, unfortunately, from people who might be able to help. Second, even if these managers went to their bosses for guidance, they'd most likely receive inadequate coaching. That's because most supervisors, riding their own long wave of hard-won successes, lack the empathy to intervene effectively. They may not know how to counsel direct reports they feel aren't quite as talented as they were at escaping the shadow of defeat. They may be so well accustomed to handling adversity in ways that minimize their psychological stress that they don't recognize their own bad habits. (See the sidebar "Coaching Resilience.")

The Capacity for Resilience

Independent studies in psychology and our own observations suggest that the ability to bounce back from adversity hinges on uncovering and untangling one's implicit beliefs about it—and shifting how one responds.

Most of us, when we experience a difficult episode, make quick assumptions about its causes, magnitude, consequences, and duration. We instantly decide, for example, whether it was inevitable, a function of forces beyond our control, or whether we could somehow have prevented it. Managers need to shift from this kind of reflexive thinking to "active" thinking about how best to respond, asking themselves what aspects they can control, what impact they can have, and how the breadth and duration of the crisis might be contained. Three types of questions can help them make this shift.

Specifying questions help managers identify ways to intervene; the more specific the answers, the better. *Visualizing questions* help shift their attention away from the adverse event and toward a more positive outcome. *Collaborating questions* push them to reach out to others—not for affirmation or commiseration but for joint problem solving. Each type of question can clarify each of the four lenses of resilient thinking.

Taken together, the four sets make up the resilience regimen. Let's take a closer look at each set in turn.

Control

According to multiple studies—including those by Bernard Weiner, of UCLA, and James Amirkhan, of Cal State Long Beach, and the classic University of Chicago study of executives by Suzanne Ouellette and Salvatore Maddi—our reactions to stressful

A change in mindset

To strengthen their resilience, managers need to shift from reflexive, cause-oriented thinking to active, response-oriented thinking.

Cause-oriented thinking	Response-oriented thinking
Control	
Was this adverse event inevitable, or could I have prevented it?	What features of the situation can I (even potentially) improve?
Impact	
Did I cause the adverse event, or did it result from external sources?	What sort of positive impact can I personally have on what happens next?
Breadth	
Is the underlying cause of this event specific to it or more widespread?	How can I contain the negatives of the situation and generate currently unseen positives?
Duration	
Is the underlying cause of this event enduring or temporary?	What can I do to begin addressing the problem now?

situations depend on the degree of control we believe we can exercise. Andrea struggled with whether she could still contribute meaningfully to her company or whether the sudden shifts in the economy had moved the situation beyond her control. If Greg continued to attribute criticism of his retail strategy to "scheming peers," he might fail to see what he personally could do to influence the company's long-term strategy or his own destiny. The following questions can help managers identify ways to exercise control over what happens next:

Specifying: What aspects of the situation can I directly influence to change the course of this adverse event?

Visualizing: What would the manager I most admire do in this situation?

Collaborating: Who on my team can help me, and what's the best way to engage that person or those people?

The goal in asking these questions is not to come up with a final plan of action or an immediate understanding of how the team should react. Rather, it is to generate possibilities—to develop, in a disciplined and concrete way, an inventory of what *might* be done. (The next set of questions can help managers outline what *will* be done.) Had Andrea asked herself these three questions, she might have identified an opportunity to, say, rally the company around emerging safety and fuel-efficiency devices in the industry, or to use the slowdown to perfect the company's newer, still-promising products by working more closely with major customers. Similarly, if Greg had undertaken the exercise, he might have been able to channel something his mentor once told him: "It's not about whether I'm right or wrong. It's about what's best for the company." With that in mind, Greg might have clearly seen the benefits of reaching out to his peers and team members to assess alternative go-to-market approaches. The ingenuity and work ethic he had applied to building the retail business could have been turned to devising the next great strategy.

Impact

Related to our beliefs about whether we can turn things around are our assumptions about what caused a negative event: Did the problem originate with us personally, or somewhere else? Greg attributed the criticism of his retail distribution strategy to his "competitive, power-hungry" colleagues rather than to the possible shortcomings of his approach. He was too deeply mired in defensiveness to get out of his own way. Andrea felt powerless in the face of challenges she'd never before had to meet and forces that eclipsed her individual initiative and effort. Instead of giving in to deflation and victimization, managers can focus intently on how they might affect the event's outcome.

> *Specifying:* How can I step up to make the most immediate, positive impact on this situation?
>
> *Visualizing:* What positive effect might my efforts have on those around me?
>
> *Collaborating:* How can I mobilize the efforts of those who are hanging back?

If he had focused on these questions, Greg might have seen that he was not simply being asked to discard his accounts and acknowledge that his strategy was misguided; rather, he was being cast as a potential player in the organization's change efforts. He might have appreciated that openly and rigorously assessing his business-development strategy could influence others—whether his assessment validated the status quo or led to a solution no one had thought of yet. And he might have reignited the entrepreneurial culture he so valued when he joined the company by soliciting others' input on the marketing strategy. For her part, Andrea knew all too well that her company's fortunes depended on economic conditions—but she couldn't see how her response to the market failures might energize the organization. These questions might have helped her.

Breadth

When we encounter a setback, we tend to assume that its causes are either specific to the situation or more broadly applicable, like poison that will taint everything we touch. To build up resilience, managers need to stop worrying about the reach of the causes and focus instead on how to limit the damage. These questions may even highlight opportunities in the midst of chaos.

> *Specifying:* What can I do to reduce the potential downside of this adverse event—by even 10%? What can I do to maximize the potential upside—by even 10%?
>
> *Visualizing:* What strengths and resources will my team and I develop by addressing this event?
>
> *Collaborating:* What can each of us do on our own, and what can we do collectively, to contain the damage and transform the situation into an opportunity?

These questions might have helped Andrea achieve two core objectives. Instead of endlessly revisiting the repercussions of plummeting truck sales, she might have identified large and small ways in which she and her team could use the economic crisis to reconfigure the company's manufacturing processes. And rather than fixating on how awful and extensive the damage to the organization was, she could have imagined a new postrecession norm—thriving in the face of tighter resources, more selective customers, and more exacting government scrutiny. Greg might have seen that he had a rare opportunity to gain valuable leadership skills and relevant insights about competitors' marketing strategies by engaging peers and team members in reassessing the retail strategy.

Duration

Some hardships in the workplace seem to have no end in sight—underperformance quarter after quarter, recurring clashes between people at different levels and in different parts of the company, a stalled economy. But questions about duration can put the brakes on such runaway nightmares. Here, though, it's important to begin by imagining the desired outcome.

Visualizing: What do I want life to look like on the other side of this adversity?

Specifying: What can I do in the next few minutes, or hours, to move in that direction?

Collaborating: What sequence of steps can we put together as a team, and what processes can we develop and adopt, to see us through to the other side of this hardship?

Greg was sure that criticism of his business-development approach signaled the end: no more promotions, no more recognition from higher-ups of his hard work and tangible results, nothing to look forward to but doing others' bidding in a company that was sowing the seeds of decline. These three questions might have broadened his outlook. That is, he might have seen the benefits of quickly arranging meetings with his mentor (for personal counsel) and with his team (for professional input on strategy). The questions could have been a catalyst for listing the data required to make a case for or against change, the analyses the team would need to run, and the questions about various sales channels and approaches that needed to be answered. This exercise might have helped Greg see a workable path through the challenge he was experiencing. The result would have been renewed confidence that he and his team could keep their company at the forefront of customer service.

Answering the Questions

Although the question sets offer a useful framework for retraining managers' responses, simply knowing what to ask isn't enough. You won't become more resilient simply because you've read this far and have made a mental note to pull out these questions the next time a destabilizing difficulty strikes. To strengthen your capacity for resilience, you need to internalize the questions by following two simple precepts:

Write down the answers

Various studies on stress and coping with trauma demonstrate that the act of writing about difficult episodes can enhance an individual's emotional and physical well-being. Indeed, writing offers people command over an adverse situation in a way that merely thinking about it does not. It's best to treat the resilience regimen as a timed exercise: Give yourself at least 15 minutes, uninterrupted, to write down your responses to the 12 questions. That may seem both too long and too short—too long because managers rarely have that much time for any activity, let alone one involving personal reflection. But you'll actually end up saving time. Instead of ruminating about events, letting them interrupt your work, you'll have solutions in the making. As you come to appreciate and rely on this exercise, 15 minutes may feel too short.

Do it every day

When you're learning any new skill, repetition is critical. The resilience regimen is a long-term fitness plan, not a crash diet. You must ask and answer these questions daily if they are to become second nature. But that can't happen if bad habits crowd out the questions. You don't need to experience a major trauma to practice; you can ask yourself the questions in response to daily annoyances that sap your energy—a delayed flight, a slow computer, an unresponsive colleague. You can use the four lenses in virtually any order, but it's important to start with your weakest dimension. If you tend to blame others and overlook your own potential to contribute, start with the impact questions. If you tend to worry that the adverse event will ruin everything, start with the breadth questions.

. . .

Under ongoing duress, executives' capacity for resilience is critical to maintaining their mental and physical health. Paradoxically, however, building resilience is best done precisely when times are most difficult—when we face the most upending challenges, when we are at the greatest risk of misfiring with our reactions, when we are blindest to the opportunities presented. All the more reason, then, to use the resilience regimen to tamp down unproductive responses to adversity, replace negativity with creativity and resourcefulness, and get things done despite real or perceived obstacles.

Originally published in January–February 2010. Reprint R1001E

How to Overcome Your Fear of the Unknown

by Nathan Furr and
Susannah Harmon Furr

Humans are wired to fear the unknown. That's why uncertainty—whether at the macro level of a global economic, health, or geopolitical crisis or at the micro level (Will I get that job? Will this venture be successful? Am I on the right career path?)—can feel nerve-racking, exhausting, and even debilitating. However, that gut reaction leads people to miss a crucial fact: Uncertainty and possibility are two sides of the same coin.

Consider the achievements you're most proud of, the moments that transformed your life, the relationships that make your life worth living. We'll bet that they all happened after a period of uncertainty—one that probably felt stressful but that you nevertheless pushed through to accomplish something great. When we moved abroad, for example, we faced uncertainty about making less money, paying higher taxes, doing more-challenging work, and introducing our children to new schools, a new language, and a new culture. But seven years later we are so grateful for all the possibilities the move opened up.

Our modern-day heroes all have a similar story. Rosa Parks faced great uncertainty when she refused to give up her seat, igniting the Montgomery bus boycott and paving the way for desegregation. Nearly everyone initially thought that Elon Musk and his team would fail when they set out to revolutionize electric vehicles and push the world toward a more environmentally friendly future. They couldn't have achieved their breakthroughs if they had been afraid of uncertainty.

Uncertainty doesn't have to paralyze any of us. Over the past decade we have studied innovators and changemakers who've learned to navigate it well, and we've reviewed the research on topics like resilience and tolerance for ambiguity. The findings are clear: We all can become adept at managing uncertainty and empower ourselves to step confidently into the unknown and seize the opportunity it presents. Applying the following four principles will help you do that.

1. Reframe Your Situation

Most people are loss-averse. Multiple studies demonstrate that the way you frame things affects how you make decisions. The research shows, for instance, that if one treatment for a new disease is described as 95% effective and another as 5% ineffective, people prefer the former even though the two are statistically identical. Every innovation, every change, every transformation—personal or professional—comes with potential upsides and downsides. And though most of us instinctively focus on the latter, it's possible to shift that mindset and decrease our fear.

Idea in Brief

The Problem

Humans are naturally wired to fear the unknown, leading to stress and anxiety that often prevents them from seizing opportunities and achieving their professional potential.

The Solution

Four principles can help you manage and embrace uncertainty: reframing situations to see potential upsides, priming yourself for new risks by maintaining certain routines, taking small actionable steps to learn and adapt, and sustaining yourself by recasting setbacks.

The Benefits

By applying these principles, you can transform uncertainty into opportunities, leading to personal growth and success. This article provides examples of innovators and change makers who have navigated uncertainty and the unknown effectively.

One of our favorite ways of doing this is the "infinite game" approach, developed by New York University professor James Carse. His advice is to stop seeing the rules, boundaries, and purpose of the "game" you're playing—the job you're after, the project you've been assigned, the career path you're on—as fixed. That puts you in a win-or-lose mentality in which uncertainty heightens your anxiety. In contrast, infinite players recognize uncertainty as an essential part of the game—one that adds an element of surprise and possibility and enables them to challenge their roles and the game's parameters.

Yvon Chouinard, the cofounder of Patagonia, is an infinite player. As a kid he struggled to fit in, running away from one school, almost failing out of a second, and becoming a "dirtbag" climber after he graduated. But rather than seeing himself as a failure, he recounts in his book *Let My People Go Surfing*, he "learned at an early age that it's better to invent your own game; then you can always be a winner."

Chouinard not only created one of the world's most successful outdoor-apparel brands but also changed production norms by adopting more-sustainable materials, altered the retail model by refitting old buildings for new shops, and challenged traditional HR policies by introducing practices like on-site childcare. Some of those innovations created uncertainty for the business. For example, Patagonia adopted organic cotton before it became popular, when it was expensive and hard to source. When a financial downturn hit, outsiders encouraged the company to buy cheaper materials. But using organic cotton was in keeping with its values, so Patagonia persisted, despite the cost and the supply risks, and in the end grew its sales while its competitors saw their sales fall.

Chouinard has learned to face uncertainty with courage—and in fact to be energized by it—because he views his role as improving the game, not just playing it. "Managers of a business that want to be around for the next 100 years had better love change," he advises in his book. "When there [is] no crisis, the wise leader . . . will invent one."

Of course, when uncertainty is forced upon us, we often need help reframing. Consider Amy and Michael, a professional couple with four children who moved from the United States to France in 2017 for Michael's job. When the pandemic started, his position was eliminated, and then companies that initially promised him job offers started stalling. In July 2020, Amy and Michael were scheduled to fly home to the United States, but three days before they left they still didn't have jobs or even a place to live. Family and friends were asking for updates, and their teenagers harangued them: "You are the worst parents ever! How can you have no clue where we're going next?"

Two days before their flight, Amy confided to us over lunch that Michael had been offered a job, but neither of them wanted him to accept it. "Should we just take the bird in hand?" she wondered aloud. "I feel like we are such losers." We encouraged her to reframe. She and Michael were showing resilience and bravery by exploring all possible next steps and holding out for the right one. How lucky their kids were to have parents bold enough to know what they really wanted and wait for it! The couple returned to the States with curiosity and courage and, by summer's end, had both found jobs they loved as well as a fixer-upper home in a fun location.

2. Prime Yourself for New Risks

Although innovators often talk about eating uncertainty for breakfast, if you dig deeper, you discover some curious habits. When Paul Smith—a designer known for daring color combinations—travels, he always stays in the same hotel, often in the same room. Others we've studied book the same airplane seat for every flight, follow the same morning routine, or wear the same clothes. Steve Jobs had a lifetime supply of black turtlenecks.

All those habits provide balance. By reducing uncertainty in one part of your life, they prime you to tolerate more of it in other parts. Some people ground themselves with steady, long-term relationships, for instance. As the serial entrepreneur Sam Yagan, one of *Time*'s 100 most influential people and the former CEO of Match.com explains, "My best friends are from junior high and high school. I married my high school sweetheart. Given how much ambiguity I traffic in at work, I do look for less in other areas of my life."

You can also prime yourself for uncertainty by getting to know the kinds of risk you have a natural aversion to or an affinity with. Case in point: Back when Nathan was pursuing a PhD in Silicon Valley and Susannah had started a clothing line that wasn't yet making money, we had four children to support and were still living off student loans in a few hundred square feet of on-campus housing. At lunch one day, Nathan told his mentor, Tina Seelig, "Let's face it, if I really had any courage, I would become an entrepreneur, but I'm just not a risk-taker." Tina disagreed. She explained that there are many types of risks: financial, intellectual, social, emotional, physical, and so on. In Nathan's situation, avoiding financial risk by pursuing a stable career as an academic—while still taking intellectual risks—was a prudent choice. The important lesson is that knowing which risks you tolerate well can help you see where to push more boldly into the frontier, while knowing which you don't will help you prepare so that you can approach them with more confidence.

Just as important, you can increase your risk tolerance by taking smaller risks, even in unrelated fields. Consider Piet Coelewij, a former senior executive at Amazon and Philips. When he was thinking of leaving the corporate track to head the expansion of Sonos—then a startup—in Europe, he decided to take up kickboxing. Coelewij describes himself as "naturally fearful of physical confrontation," but trying kickboxing helped him build up his muscles for dealing with uncertainty, which made him "more comfortable with higher-risk decisions in other settings with less complete information," he says. "Once you are in a cycle of lowering fear and developing courage, you create a virtuous circle that allows you to continuously improve."

3. Do Something

Taking action is one of the most important parts of facing uncertainty, since you learn with each step you take. Research by Timothy Ott and Kathleen Eisenhardt demonstrates that most successful breakthroughs are produced by a series of small steps, not giant bet-the-farm efforts. Starting modestly can be more effective and less anxiety-provoking than trying to do everything at once.

When Jenn Hyman and Jenny Fleiss, the founders of Rent the Runway, first had the idea of renting out designer dresses online, they were students at Harvard Business School. But they didn't begin by writing a business plan, raising money, and then getting big as fast as possible. Instead they made one small move: They rustled up some dresses, set up a dressing room on Harvard's campus before a big dance, and observed firsthand whether women would rent them. Then, one experiment after another, one step at a time, they built a large, successful public company.

Sometimes you need to quickly ramp up your learning to blow away the fog that obscures the view of what to do next. Entrepreneurs face that challenge all the time. Research on the most-effective startup accelerators demonstrates that the best way to help founders meet it is to make them talk with as many people, from as many different backgrounds, as quickly as possible (instead of keeping their ideas to themselves for fear that someone might steal them). Leading accelerators often force entrepreneurs to meet more than 200 people, some from seemingly unrelated backgrounds, in just one month.

It's not unusual for invaluable input to come from unexpected corners. The founder of one new platform dedicated to helping charities, including religious organizations, initially balked at the feedback session his accelerator had arranged with the vice president of marketing at *Playboy*. To his shock, the VP not only was a churchgoer but also gave him some of the most helpful advice he had received so far.

Finally, as you make your way forward, focus on values rather than on goals. David Heinemeier Hansson, the creator of Ruby on Rails and the cofounder of multiple startups, including Basecamp and Hey.com, views goals as "oppressive" and argues that setting them doesn't even work. "Whether you meet $10 million or not does not happen because you set that as a goal," he explains. If you instead aim to fulfill your values (which for him include coding great software, treating employees well, and acting ethically in the market), you'll have the confidence to make the moves you need to, no matter how the world responds, because you've redefined what success means to you. Even if a big project fails, he says, "I will still look back on the path—the two years and millions of dollars we spent developing this thing—and feel great about it."

He took that approach when Apple began imposing exorbitant app store fees on his most recent project, Hey.com, threatening to shut the new email service down just after it launched. He admits that even he felt anxiety about the uncertainty, just as anyone else would. But his focus on values, rather than goals—in particular, on fairness in the tech industry—"gave us freedom to go all in" fighting back, he says. His situation became a rallying point for entrepreneurs, and the free press that resulted became "the greatest launch campaign we could have imagined."

4. Sustain Yourself

According to Ben Feringa, who won a Nobel Prize in chemistry for work on molecular machines that could one day power nanobots that repair the pipes in your house or keep diseases out of your blood, scientific discovery happens only after facing uncertainty. That means, he says, you have to "get resilient at handling the frustration that comes with it." His approach includes both emotional hygiene (attending to emotions—much as you would a physical wound—so that they don't turn into paralyzing self-doubt or unproductive rumination) and reality checks (in which you recognize that failure is just part of the process).

Feringa admits that failing hurts and that he allows himself to feel frustrated, even for a few days. But then he stops and asks, What insights can I take away from this? What's the next step I can work on? Whether he realizes it or not, he's adopting one of many lenses that can help people recast setbacks, such as the learning lens (what you can learn from them), the gratitude lens (what you still have, not what you lost), the timing lens (it's just not the right time now, but that doesn't mean it won't ever be), and our favorite: the challenge lens (you become the hero only by facing obstacles).

Another practice that the scientists, creators, and entrepreneurs we've studied use to sustain themselves is to focus on the people and things that have meaning for them. You can get through anything—not just the fear of potential losses but the pain of real ones—by holding tight to what really matters.

Take Jos and Alison Skeates, a British couple who launched a small chain of jewelry shops featuring new designers. They'd opened locations in three London neighborhoods—Clerkenwell,

Notting Hill, and Chiswick—all while raising their two young girls. Then a series of disasters struck. First, construction around the Notting Hill store killed foot traffic. Then the financial crisis of 2008 crushed sales and, much worse, Alison was diagnosed with an aggressive form of cancer. They had to close two shops and declare bankruptcy. But they navigated those tragedies by remembering that their love and their family were more important than the business.

Slowly, Alison's health improved and the cancer went into remission. Eventually they relaunched the Clerkenwell shop, repaid all their former creditors, and even won an award for being the UK jewelry boutique of the year. They also discovered a new, more meaningful pursuit: becoming one of the UK's first certified B-corp jewelry workshops, leading the way in sustainable practices.

Ultimately, their switch to sustainable jewelry strengthened them and their business. Recently, Jos went back to school to earn a master's degree in sustainability. More than 30 years out of school, he seriously doubted whether he could meet the rigorous reading and writing demands of the program while still running the store. The upside to this uncertainty? "What I have learned has been so interesting and inspiring, and our sales have increased," he says. Although he and Alison didn't build the chic jewelry empire they had imagined, their lives are happier and richer on this side of many challenges.

. . .

Resilience—being able to take a blow and stay standing—is important. But we argue for something more: learning to transform uncertainty into opportunity. The only way for any of us to tap into new possibilities is through the gateway of the unknown. And it doesn't have to be a painful process if you believe in your ability to navigate it. Our hope is that you can use our advice to transform your relationship with change and inspire others to do the same.

Originally published July–August 2022. Reprint R2204L

QUICK READ

How to Stop Worrying About What Other People Think of You

by Michael Gervais

If you want to be your best and perform at a high level, your fear of people's opinions may be holding you back.

Think about a time when you were extremely anxious—say, before standing up to speak in public, raising your hand in a big meeting, or even walking through a room of strangers. The reason you felt small, scared, and tense is you were worried about social disapproval.

Our fear of other people's opinions, or FOPO as I call it, has become an irrational and unproductive obsession in the modern world, and its negative effects reach far beyond performance.

If you start paying less and less attention to what makes you *you*—your talents, beliefs, and values—and start conforming to what others may or *may not* think, you'll harm your potential. You'll start playing it safe because you're afraid of what will happen on the other side of the critique. You'll fear being ridiculed or rejected. When challenged, you'll surrender your viewpoint.

You won't raise your hand when you can't control the outcome. You won't go for that promotion because you'll think you're unqualified.

Unfortunately, FOPO is part of the human condition because we're operating with an ancient brain. A craving for social approval made our ancestors cautious and savvy; thousands of years ago, if the responsibility for the failed hunt fell on your shoulders, your place in the tribe could be threatened. The desire to fit in and the paralyzing fear of being disliked undermine our ability to pursue the lives we want to create.

This underscores why we need to train and condition our mind—so the tail is not wagging the dog.

If you find yourself experiencing FOPO, there are ways to dampen the intensity of your stress responses. Once you're aware of your thoughts, guide yourself toward confidence-building statements (I am a good public speaker; I've put in the work so that I can trust my abilities; I have a lot of great things to say; I'm completely prepared for this promotion). These statements will help you focus on your skills and abilities rather than others' opinions. Take deep breaths, too. This will signal to your brain that you're not in immediate danger.

But, if you really want to conquer FOPO, you'll need to cultivate more self-awareness. Most of us go through life with a general sense of who we are, and in a lot of circumstances, that's enough. We get by. But if you want to be your best while being less fearful of people's opinions, you need to develop a stronger and much deeper sense of who you are.

You can start by developing a personal philosophy—a word or phrase that expresses your basic beliefs and values. The personal philosophy of Pete Carroll, my business partner and longtime NFL head coach, is "always compete." For Coach Carroll, always

Idea In Brief

The Problem

Fear of other people's opinions (FOPO) often leads to anxiety and stress, which can hold you back from performing your best and pursuing opportunities. FOPO is deeply ingrained in human nature due to our ancient brain's craving for social approval.

The Solution

To overcome FOPO, you should develop self-awareness and look at your personal philosophy. By focusing on your talents, beliefs, and values, and crafting guiding principles, you can navigate social disapproval more effectively. Techniques like confidence-building statements and deep breathing can also help manage stress responses.

The Benefits

Reducing FOPO can lead to personal and professional growth. High performers who have a clear sense of their guiding principles are more willing to push themselves, learn, and embrace discomfort, leading to a more fulfilling and purposeful life.

---

competing means spending every day working hard to get better and reach his fullest potential. This philosophy isn't a platitude or slogan; rather, it's his compass, guiding his actions, thoughts, and decisions. As a coach. A father. A friend. In every area of life.

When coming up with a personal philosophy, ask yourself a series of questions:

> *When I'm at my best, what beliefs lie just beneath the surface of my thoughts and actions?*

> *Who are people that demonstrate characteristics and qualities that are aligned with mine?*

> *What are those qualities?*

> *What are your favorite quotes? Your favorite words?*

Once you've answered these questions, circle the words that stand out to you and cross out the ones that don't. After studying what's left, try to come up with a phrase or sentence that lines up with exactly who you are and how you want to live your life. Share the draft with a loved one, ask for input, and fine-tune your philosophy from there. Then commit it to memory and return to it daily.

Crafting a personal philosophy can be an eye-opening and powerful exercise. When I coach teams of executives, I often ask them to write down their personal philosophy and share it with the group. I'll never forget the time a senior executive wowed everyone in the room. As tears welled up in his eyes, he straightened his back, held his head high, and said, "My philosophy is to walk worthy." He told his colleagues that his parents were immigrants who had persevered through challenging circumstances to ensure he had better opportunities. Because of his parents' hard work and sacrifice, he considered it his duty to live life as if his family crest were emblazoned across his chest. Every day, he tries to be worthy of their good deeds, and to be a great role model for the next generation.

I can't overstate how important a personal philosophy is. Working with NFL players and coaches, extreme-sport athletes, and senior leaders at *Fortune* 50 companies, I've noticed that, beyond a relentless pursuit of being their best, what makes these high performers great is their clear sense of the principles that guide them. Because of their clarity, they're more willing to push themselves, learn more, and embrace discomfort. They can shut out the noise and opinions of fans and media and listen to their own well-calibrated, internal compass.

Once you've developed your own personal philosophy, commit yourself to live in accordance with its tenets. Start at home.

Tell that person you love them. Dance at a wedding. Take risks. Be respectfully weird. (That probably means, be you.) Then try it at work. Give a presentation. Go for that promotion. Do things that will engender the opinions of others. When you feel the power of FOPO holding you back, simply acknowledge it and reconnect to your philosophy and the larger objective at hand.

Moving forward, solicit feedback from a short list of people who matter to you. Honest reflection is a vital component of mastery. During an episode of my podcast *Finding Mastery*, Brené Brown, a renowned researcher and author of *Dare to Lead*, suggested that the names of those people should fit on a 1 × 1-inch index card. I add a second condition. The people on your card should have a great sense of the person you are and the person you're working to become. Hold their views in high regard, letting the noise from the crowd fade away. Calibrate their feedback with your experience.

Most of all, remember that growth and learning take place when you're operating at the edge of your capacity. Like blowing up a nearly inflated balloon, living in accordance with your personal philosophy will require more effort and power, but the result, which is to authentically and artistically express who you are, will push you to live and work with more purpose and meaning.

Adapted from hbr.org, May 2, 2019. Reprint H04XBL

Give Yourself a Break: The Power of Self-Compassion

by Serena Chen

When people experience a setback at work—whether it's a bad sales quarter, being overlooked for a promotion, or an interpersonal conflict with a colleague—it's common to respond in one of two ways. Either we become defensive and blame others, or we berate ourselves. Unfortunately, neither response is especially helpful. Shirking responsibility by getting defensive may alleviate the sting of failure, but it comes at the expense of learning. Self-flagellation, on the other hand, may feel warranted in the moment, but it can lead to an inaccurately gloomy assessment of one's potential, which undermines personal development.

What if instead we were to treat ourselves as we would a friend in a similar situation? More likely than not, we'd be kind, understanding, and encouraging. Directing that type of response internally, toward ourselves, is known as self-compassion, and it's been the focus of a good deal of research in recent years. Psychologists are discovering that self-compassion is a useful tool for enhancing performance in a variety of settings, from healthy aging to athletics. I and other researchers have begun focusing on how self-compassion also enhances professional growth.

For nonacademics, self-compassion is a less familiar concept than self-esteem or self-confidence. Although it's true that people who engage in self-compassion tend to have higher self-esteem, the two concepts are distinct. Self-esteem tends to involve evaluating oneself in comparison with others. Self-compassion, on the other hand, doesn't involve judging the self or others. Instead, it creates a sense of self-worth because it leads people to genuinely care about their own well-being and recovery after a setback.

People with high levels of self-compassion demonstrate three behaviors: First, they are kind rather than judgmental about their own failures and mistakes; second, they recognize that failures are a shared human experience; and third, they take a balanced approach to negative emotions when they stumble or fall short—they allow themselves to feel bad, but they don't let negative emotions take over.

Kristin Neff, a professor at the University of Texas, Austin, has developed a survey tool that assesses the three components of self-compassion. Researchers and practitioners have used the tool to shed light on what personality traits and behaviors are associated with self-compassion and have found, among other things, that people who score high typically have greater motivation to improve themselves and are more likely to report strong feelings of authenticity—the sense of being true to the self. Both are important contributors to a successful career. The

Idea in Brief

The Problem
When people experience setbacks or make mistakes at work, they often respond by either blaming others or berating themselves. Both responses are unhelpful; they prevent learning and can lead to an inaccurately negative self-assessment, slowing your personal and professional growth.

The Solution
Self-compassion means treating yourself with kindness, recognizing that failures are a shared human experience, and maintaining a balanced approach to negative emotions. Using it will help you develop a realistic appraisal of yourself, adopt a growth mindset, and improve your motivation.

The Benefits
Embracing self-compassion can lead to better performance and a greater sense of connection with your authentic self. Leaders can enhance their ability to manage by example and create a positive work environment.

---

good news is that both of these traits can be cultivated and enhanced through self-compassion.

A Growth Mindset

Most organizations and people want to improve—and self-compassion is crucial for that. We tend to associate personal growth with determination, persistence, and hard work, but the process often starts with reflection. One of the key requirements for self-improvement is having a realistic assessment of where we stand—of our strengths and our limitations. Convincing ourselves that we are better than we are leads to complacency, and thinking we're worse than we are leads to defeatism. When people treat themselves with compassion, they are better able to arrive at realistic self-appraisals, which is the foundation for improvement. They are also more motivated to work on their weaknesses rather than think "What's the point?" and to summon the grit required to enhance skills and change bad habits.

My colleagues Juliana Breines (at the University of Rhode Island) and Jia Wei Zhang (at the University of Memphis) and I demonstrated this in a series of studies in which participants were nudged to treat themselves either with self-compassion or in a self-esteem-boosting manner. Then we assessed their desire for self-improvement. In one study, we asked participants to recall a time when they did something they felt was wrong and as a result experienced guilt, remorse, and regret. The majority of participants' transgressions involved romantic infidelity, academic misconduct, dishonesty, betrayal of trust, or hurting someone they cared about. We then randomly assigned them to one of three conditions: self-compassion, self-esteem, or a control group. The self-compassion participants were asked to write a paragraph to themselves expressing kindness and understanding regarding the transgression. The self-esteem people were asked to write a paragraph describing their positive qualities. Participants in the control group were asked to write about a hobby they enjoyed. All participants then filled out a questionnaire assessing their desire to make amends and their commitment not to repeat the transgression in the future. We found that those who were encouraged to treat themselves with compassion reported being more motivated to make amends and to never repeat the transgression than participants who were encouraged to respond to the transgression in a self-esteem-boosting manner and those in the control group. In other research, we found that self-compassion increased the resolve of people who said they had been responsible for a romantic breakup to be better partners in future relationships, compared with participants in the other two conditions.

Self-compassion does more than help people recover from failure or setbacks. It also supports what Carol Dweck, a psychology professor at Stanford University, has called a "growth mindset." Dweck has documented the benefits of adopting a growth rather than "fixed" approach to performance, whether it be in launching a successful startup, parenting, or running a marathon. People with a fixed mindset see personality traits and abilities, including their own, as set in stone. They believe that who we are today is essentially who we'll be five years from now. People who have a growth mindset, in contrast, view personality traits and abilities as malleable. They see the potential for growth and thus are more likely to try to improve—to put in effort and practice and to stay positive and optimistic.

My research suggests that self-compassion triggers people to adopt a growth mindset. In one study I conducted with Juliana Breines, participants were asked to identify what they considered to be their biggest weakness—most involved social difficulties such as lack of confidence, anxiety, shyness, and insecurity in relationships—after which they were randomly assigned to one of three groups. Participants in the self-compassion group were asked to write a response to this prompt: "Imagine that you are talking to yourself about this weakness from a compassionate and understanding perspective. What would you say?" People in the self-esteem group were asked to write in response to: "Imagine that you are talking to yourself about this weakness from a perspective of validating your positive (rather than negative) qualities." The final group was not asked to write anything.

Next, participants completed a set of measures about whether they felt content, sad, or upset and then were asked to spend five minutes describing whether they've ever done anything to change their weakness and where they thought their weakness came from. Independent coders rated participants' responses based on the degree to which they conveyed a growth or a fixed mindset ("It's just inborn—there's nothing I can do" versus "With hard work I know I can change"). Participants in the self-compassion condition expressed significantly more thoughts associated with a growth mindset than participants in the other two conditions.

But what about actual behavior? How do we know that self-compassion—and the resulting growth mindset—will lead people to work harder to improve themselves? According to the scientific literature on fixed and growth mindsets, one of the most compelling signs that a person has a growth mindset is his or her willingness to keep trying to do better after receiving negative feedback. After all, if you believe your abilities are fixed, there's no point in making the effort. But if you view abilities as changeable, getting negative feedback shouldn't deter you in trying to improve.

We tested this reasoning in a study in which participants (all students at a highly ranked university) first took a very difficult vocabulary test and received feedback that they had performed poorly. The participants were then randomly assigned to two groups. The experimenter remarked to the first group—the self-compassion condition—"If you had difficulty with the test you just took, you're not alone. It's common for students to have difficulty with tests like this. If you feel bad about how you did, try not to be too hard on yourself." To the other group of participants, the experimenter instead said: "If you had difficulty with the test you just took, try not to feel bad about yourself—you must be intelligent if you got into this university."

Afterward, all participants were told they had to take another vocabulary test. They were given a chance to study a list of words and definitions and were advised that they could review the words as long they wanted before taking the test. We found that participants who were nudged to treat their initial failure with compassion were more likely to adopt a growth mindset about their vocabulary abilities and put in more time studying than their counterparts in the self-esteem condition were. It seems that self-compassion paved the way for self-improvement by revving up their desire to do better, encouraging the belief that improvement is possible, and motivating them to work harder.

Being True to the Self

Self-compassion has benefits for the workplace beyond boosting employees' drive to improve. Over time, it can help people gravitate to roles that better fit their personality and values. Living in accord with one's true self—what psychologists term "authenticity"—results in increased motivation and drive (along with a host of other mental health benefits). Unfortunately, authenticity remains elusive for many in the workplace. People may feel stuck in jobs where they have to suppress their true self because of incongruent workplace norms around behavior, doubts about what they have to contribute, or fears about being judged negatively by colleagues and superiors. But self-compassion can help people assess their professional and personal trajectories and make course corrections when and where necessary. A self-compassionate sales executive who misses a quarterly target, for example, not only will focus on how she can make her numbers next quarter but also will be more likely to take stock of whether she is in the right sort of job for her temperament and disposition.

In recent research spearheaded by Jia Wei Zhang, we discovered that self-compassion cultivates authenticity by minimizing negative thoughts and self-doubts. In an initial study, participants completed a short survey on a daily basis for one week. They were asked to rate their levels of self-compassion ("Today, I showed caring, understanding, and kindness toward myself") and authenticity ("Today, I felt authentic and genuine in my interactions with others") each day. We found that daily variations in levels of self-compassion were closely linked to variations in feelings of authenticity. On days when participants reported being more compassionate toward themselves relative to their average level, they also reported greater feelings of authenticity.

These correlational findings were strengthened by experimental evidence from another study in which we randomly assigned participants to respond to a personal weakness from a self-compassionate perspective, a self-esteem-boosting perspective, or neither. Immediately afterward, they completed questionnaires that measured how authentic they felt. Participants who were instructed to be self-compassionate about their weakness reported significantly higher feelings of authenticity than participants in the other two conditions did.

What's happening here? Treating oneself with kindness, understanding, and without judgment alleviates fears about social disapproval, paving the way for authenticity. Optimism also seems to play a role. Having a positive outlook on life makes people more willing to take chances—such as revealing their true selves. In fact, research shows that optimistic people are more likely to reveal negative things about themselves—such as distressing experiences they've endured or difficult medical challenges they face. In effect, optimism increases people's inclination to be authentic, despite the potential risks involved. I believe that the relative emotional calm and the balanced perspective that come with being self-compassionate can help people approach difficult experiences with a positive attitude.

Turbocharged Leadership

A self-compassionate mindset produces benefits that spread to others, too. This is especially the case for people in leadership roles. That's because self-compassion and compassion for others are linked: Practicing one boosts the other. Being kind and nonjudgmental toward the self is good practice for treating others compassionately, just as compassion for others can increase how compassionate people are toward themselves, creating an upward cycle of compassion—and an antidote to "incivility spirals" that too often plague work environments.

The fact that self-compassion encourages a growth mindset is also relevant here. Research shows that when leaders adopt a growth mindset (that is, believe that change is possible), they're more likely to pay attention to changes in subordinates' performance and to give useful feedback on how to improve. Subordinates, in turn, can discern when their leaders have growth mindsets, which makes them more motivated and satisfied, not to mention more likely to adopt growth mindsets themselves. The old adage "lead by example" applies to self-compassion and the growth mindset it encourages.

A similar link between leader and subordinates exists for authenticity, too. People can sense authenticity in others, and when leaders are seen as being true to themselves, it creates an atmosphere of authenticity throughout the workplace. There's also substantial evidence that stronger relationships are forged when people feel authentic in their interactions with others.

When leaders respond to failures and setbacks with a self-compassionate attitude, they themselves benefit, being more likely to exhibit psychological and behavioral tendencies that bode well for their own professional development and success. And the benefits can trickle down to subordinates, making the practice of self-compassion a win-win for leaders and those they lead.

Fostering Self-Compassion

Fostering self-compassion is not complicated or difficult. It's a skill that can be learned and enhanced. For the analytically minded, I suggest using psychologists' definition of self-compassion as a three-point checklist: Am I being kind and understanding to myself? Do I acknowledge shortcomings and failure as experiences shared by everyone? Am I keeping my negative feelings in perspective? If this doesn't work, a simple "trick" can also help: Sit down and write yourself a letter in the third person, as if you were a friend or loved one. Many of us are better at being a good friend to other people than to ourselves, so this can help avoid spirals of defensiveness or self-flagellation.

The business community at large has done a good job of removing the stigma around failure in recent years at the organizational level—it's a natural byproduct of experimentation and, ultimately, innovation. But too many of us are not harnessing the redemptive power of failure in our own work lives. As more and more industries are disrupted and people's work lives are thrown into upheaval, this skill will become more important.

If you're struggling to foster self-compassion in your professional and personal life, don't beat yourself up about it. With a little practice, you can do better.

Originally published in September–October 2018. Reprint R1805J

QUICK READ

How to Stop Dwelling on Your Stress

by Jenny Taitz

Wouldn't it be nice if we could learn to put our stressors aside from time to time, at least temporarily? I'm not talking about meditating or simply calming down, the latter of which isn't even possible sometimes, given the world we live in now. I'm talking about changing our thinking and breaking the stress cycle, which *is* possible.

As a clinical psychologist who specializes in mindfulness-based behavioral therapies, I've found that many of my clients engage in what stress researchers call "perseverative cognition," which is a fancy phrase for overthinking, ruminating, and worrying. And while it's easy to imagine that this kind of thinking can better prepare us to handle stress, science suggests that it actually turns acute stress (the way we respond to a single, discrete event or situation) into prolonged stress, since we're taking something fleeting and prolonging it unnecessarily.

When people are asked to think about something that incensed them, even if it occurred decades ago, the body reexperiences the full impact of the event, which spikes blood pressure in real time, according to research done at Penn State University.[1] Another way we keep stressors top of mind is when we endlessly vent our frustrations. Since perseverative cognition recreates all the tension that went along with past woes, it's no wonder the habit links distressing events with the tolls of chronic stress.[2]

The good news is that improving your ability to stay present can allow you to set aside stressful issues that you can't immediately solve, whether it's a nagging problem at work or a personal conflict. "You can have chronic stressors that don't have a lifelong impact, and you can have acute stressors that do have a lifelong impact," explains psychologist George Slavich, a professor at University of California, Los Angeles, who leads the Laboratory for Stress Assessment and Research.

To inspire my clients to address an overthinking habit, I often share a story I heard from Sharon Salzberg, a *New York Times* bestselling author and meditation teacher. A man who was trekking in Nepal had a blister on his foot. As he hiked, instead of taking in his surroundings, he anticipated the blister before he took a step, experienced the twinge as he placed his foot on the ground, and then replayed the pain between steps, making the experience exponentially more unpleasant. In our own lives, we similarly can experience our stressors once or many times, instead of focusing on the peace of the current moment.

Four Strategies to Help You Take a Break from Stress

To begin to work on overthinking, and to learn to take more frequent breaks from stress, I recommend the following four strategies.

Idea in Brief

The Problem
Many people engage in perseverative cognition, which involves overthinking, ruminating, and worrying. This habit can turn acute stress into prolonged stress, as it recreates the tension associated with past events. Research shows that even thinking about past stressors can spike blood pressure in real time.

The Solution
Four strategies can break the stress cycle: anchoring yourself, taking your thoughts less seriously, sitting with uncertainty, and self-validating. These techniques help individuals stay present, create distance from unhelpful thoughts, accept the unknown, and legitimize their emotions.

The Benefits
Practicing these strategies can improve psychological flexibility and the ability to adapt to life's complexities. By being open to emotions, you can reduce the impact of stressors, enhance your well-being, and move toward what you value.

1. Anchor yourself

The next time your thinking is spinning you in the wrong direction, take a moment to feel the weight of your feet on the floor and then consider: *What am I thinking? What am I feeling in my body right now? What am I doing right now?* Then, ask yourself: *Are my thoughts helping me at this moment?*

For example, if you're running through tomorrow's agenda and the crazy day ahead as you get ready for bed, anchoring can help you catch what you're doing so that you don't work yourself into an insomnia-inducing headspace. After all, missing sleep will make it that much tougher to perform in the morning. This anchoring technique, taught in a research-based program known as the Unified Protocol, developed by David Barlow, a professor emeritus at Boston University, and his colleagues, treats conditions that can be fueled by overthinking, including depression and anxiety. Of course, anchoring takes effort and willingness, but it's a nice way to bring awareness to where you are, and it's so quick, you can do it multiple times a day.

2. Take your thoughts less seriously

At a conference I attended years ago, a leading academic whom I respected approached me and asked if I would be giving any talks. Without any hesitation, I quickly said, "Public speaking has never been my forte." To which he replied, "Did you thank your mind for that thought?" His answer made me smile; it's also a good example of this next technique.

Too often, most of what we think about ourselves isn't helpful or empowering. So rather than allowing those thoughts to feel like dictators in our lives, we can use cognitive defusion—taking thoughts less literally—to consciously create some distance and perspective from those thoughts, while taking them less seriously.

Because, after all, what are thoughts? They're merely patterns of ideas, not hard-and-fast truths. When I shared this story with a client, he brilliantly decided to sing, "What are thoughts? Thoughts can't hurt me . . . can't hurt me no more" to the tune of the Haddaway song "What Is Love?" It's hard to get stuck ruminating if you treat your thoughts less like cement and more like Play-Doh.

3. Sit with uncertainty

One of the reasons it can feel compelling to ruminate is the illusion that by running through all the disastrous possibilities in life, you'll be able to anticipate and avoid them, and ultimately be less stressed. But ironically, not being able to tolerate uncertainty actually predicts struggling with anxiety and other psychological problems.

As an alternative, I love the skill of wholeheartedly accepting whatever is right now, including the unknown. To try this, notice if you're thinking along the lines of *I need to know!* or *The worst is going to happen.* If you are, try turning to the present moment with openness and curiosity, and stop running through endless permutations as you relax your jaw, face, and hands—physical actions that make it a little easier to foster openness.

It's futile to use so much of our free time playing draining guessing games. "There are an infinite number of bad things that could possibly happen (although most are unlikely), and there is just no way a person can anticipate them all," according to Michel Dugas, a psychology professor at the University of Quebec.[3]

Accepting uncertainty may mean sitting with some amount of fear, but the alternative is trying to micromanage reality, which simply isn't possible. Accepting your emotions also makes it clear that unlike ruminating, which can keep us in its grip for hours, feelings are actually quite transient when we stay present in the moment.

4. Self-validate

Unresolved issues with the people we come across daily can easily fuel overthinking. Maybe a customer says something offensive to you, or a prospective employer ghosts you after multiple rounds of interviews and you can't confront them directly. You might be inclined to replay the event in your head—complete with your own angry responses—as a way to have the conversation you wish you could have had. I do this myself, and so do many of my clients.

Replaying an unfair situation again and again can feel like a way of justifying our distress and having a say in the matter. The problem is, those in-your-head conversations that you'll never actually have will just prolong your discomfort. Instead, try a strategy that's often used in dialectical behavior therapy known as self-validation, an approach developed by Marsha Linehan, a professor emeritus at University of Washington, in which you legitimize your emotions and move past replaying the hurtful loop. For example, you might think something like: *This isn't what I expected. Of course I feel angry and sad*, which can ease the pain a bit, rather than rehashing the injustice it of it all and keeping your distress at peak intensity.

. . .

Practice these four techniques and you'll improve your psychological flexibility, a term coined by Steven Hayes, who developed acceptance and commitment therapy. Research has shown that having psychological flexibility is a key ingredient in being able to adapt to life and all its complexities. All it takes is allowing yourself to be aware of your thoughts and open to your emotions, as you persist in moving toward what you value.

Adapted from hbr.org, January 30, 2024. Reprint H07ZG9

4

Building Resilience

by Martin E.P. Seligman

Douglas and Walter, two University of Pennsylvania MBA graduates, were laid off by their Wall Street companies 18 months ago. Both went into a tailspin: They were sad, listless, indecisive, and anxious about the future. For Douglas, the mood was transient. After two weeks he told himself, "It's not you; it's the economy going through a bad patch. I'm good at what I do, and there will be a market for my skills." He updated his résumé and sent it to a dozen New York firms, all of which rejected him. He then tried six companies in his Ohio hometown and eventually landed a position. Walter, by contrast, spiraled into hopelessness: "I got fired because I can't perform under pressure," he thought. "I'm not cut out for finance. The economy will take years to recover." Even as the market improved, he didn't look for another job; he ended up moving back in with his parents.

Douglas and Walter (actually composites based on interviewees) stand at opposite ends of the continuum of reactions to failure. The Douglases of the world bounce back after a brief period of malaise; within a year they've grown because of the experience. The Walters go from sadness to depression to a paralyzing fear of the future. Yet failure is a nearly inevitable part of work; and along with dashed romance, it is one of life's most common traumas. People like Walter are almost certain to find their careers stymied, and companies full of such employees are doomed in hard times. It is people like Douglas who rise to the top, and whom organizations must recruit and retain in order to succeed. But how can you tell who is a Walter and who is a Douglas? And can Walters become Douglases? Can resilience be measured and taught?

Thirty years of scientific research has put the answers to these questions within our reach. We have learned not only how to distinguish those who will grow after failure from those who will collapse, but also how to build the skills of people in the latter category. I have worked with colleagues from around the world to develop a program for teaching resilience. It is now being tested in an organization of 1.1 million people where trauma is more common and more severe than in any corporate setting: the U.S. Army. Its members may struggle with depression and post-traumatic stress disorder (PTSD), but thousands of them also experience post-traumatic growth. Our goal is to employ resilience training to reduce the number of those who struggle and increase the number of those who grow. We believe that businesspeople can draw lessons from this approach, particularly in times of failure and stagnation. Working with both individual soldiers (employees) and drill sergeants (managers), we are helping to create an army of Douglases who can turn their most difficult experiences into catalysts for improved performance.

Idea in Brief

Failure is one of life's most common traumas, yet people's responses to it vary widely. Some bounce back after a brief period of malaise; others descend into depression and a paralyzing fear of the future.

Thirty years of research suggests that resilience can be measured and taught—and the U.S. Army is putting that idea to the test with a program called Comprehensive Soldier Fitness. The aim of CSF is to make soldiers as fit psychologically as they are physically.

A key component of CSF is "master resilience training" for drill sergeants—a form of management training that teaches leaders how to embrace resilience and then pass it on, by building mental toughness, signature strengths, and strong relationships.

Optimism Is the Key

Although I'm now called the father of positive psychology, I came to it the long, hard way, through many years of research on failure and helplessness. In the late 1960s I was part of the team that discovered "learned helplessness." We found that dogs, rats, mice, and even cockroaches that experienced mildly painful shock over which they had no control would eventually just accept it, with no attempt to escape. It was next shown that human beings do the same thing. In an experiment published in 1975 by Donald Hiroto and me and replicated many times since, subjects are randomly divided into three groups. Those in the first are exposed to an annoying loud noise that they can stop by pushing a button in front of them. Those in the second hear the same noise but can't turn it off, though they try hard. Those in the third, the control group, hear nothing at all. Later, typically the following day, the subjects are faced with a brand-new situation that again involves noise. To turn the noise off, all they have to do is move their hands about 12 inches. The people in the first and third groups figure this out and readily learn to avoid the noise. But those in the second group typically do nothing. In phase one they failed, realized they had no control, and became passive. In phase two, expecting more failure, they don't even try to escape. They have learned helplessness.

Strangely, however, about a third of the animals and people who experience inescapable shocks or noise never become helpless. What is it about them that makes this so? Over 15 years of study, my colleagues and I discovered that the answer is optimism. We developed questionnaires and analyzed the content of verbatim speech and writing to assess "explanatory style" as optimistic or pessimistic. We discovered that people who don't give up have a habit of interpreting setbacks as temporary, local, and changeable. ("It's going away quickly; it's just this one situation, and I can do something about it.") That suggested how we might immunize people against learned helplessness, against depression and anxiety, and against giving up after failure: by teaching them to think like optimists. We created the Penn Resiliency Program, under the direction of Karen Reivich and Jane Gillham, of the University of Pennsylvania, for young adults and children. The program has been replicated in 21 diverse school settings—ranging from suburbs to inner cities, from Philadelphia to Beijing. We also created a 10-day program in which teachers learn techniques for becoming more optimistic in their own lives and how to teach those techniques to their students. We've found that it reduces depression and anxiety in the children under their care. (Another way we teach positive psychology is through the master of applied positive psychology, or MAPP, degree program, now in its sixth year at Penn.)

In November 2008, when the legendary General George W. Casey, Jr., the army chief of staff and former commander of the multinational force in Iraq, asked me what positive psychology had to say about soldiers' problems, I offered a simple answer: How human beings react to extreme adversity is normally distributed. On one end are the people who fall apart into PTSD, depression, and even suicide. In the middle are most people, who at first react with symptoms of depression and anxiety but within a month or so are, by physical and psychological measures, back where they were before the trauma. That is resilience. On the other end are people who show post-traumatic growth. They, too, first experience depression and anxiety, often exhibiting full-blown PTSD, but within a year they are better off than they were before the trauma. These are the people of whom Friedrich Nietzsche said, "That which does not kill us makes us stronger."

I told General Casey that the army could shift its distribution toward the growth end by teaching psychological skills to stop the downward spiral that often follows failure. He ordered the organization to measure resilience and teach positive psychology to create a force as fit psychologically as it is physically. This $145 million initiative, under the direction of Brigadier General Rhonda Cornum, is called Comprehensive Soldier Fitness (CSF) and consists of three components: a test for psychological fitness, self-improvement courses available following the test, and "master resilience training" (MRT) for drill sergeants. These are based on PERMA: positive emotion, engagement, relationships, meaning, and accomplishment—the building blocks of resilience and growth.

Testing for Psychological Fitness

A team led by the University of Michigan professor Christopher Peterson, author of the Values in Action signature strengths survey, created the test, called the Global Assessment Tool (GAT). It is a 20-minute questionnaire that focuses on strengths rather than weaknesses and is designed to measure four things: emotional, family, social, and spiritual fitness. All four have been credited with reducing depression and anxiety. According to research, they are the keys to PERMA.

Although individual scores are confidential, the GAT results allow test takers to choose appropriate basic or advanced courses for building resilience. The GAT also provides a common vocabulary for describing soldiers' assets. The data generated will allow the army to gauge the psychosocial fitness both of particular units and of the entire organization, highlighting positives and negatives. At this writing, more than 900,000 soldiers have taken the test. The army will compare psychological profiles with performance and medical results over time; the resulting database will enable us to answer questions like these: What specific strengths protect against PTSD, depression, anxiety, and suicide? Does a strong sense of meaning result in better performance? Are people who score high in positive emotion promoted more quickly? Can optimism spread from a leader to his troops?

Online Courses

The second component of CSF is optional online courses in each of the four fitnesses and one mandatory course on posttraumatic growth. The implications for corporate managers are more obvious for some modules than for others, but I'll briefly explain them all.

The emotional fitness module, created by Barbara Fredrickson, a professor of emotions and psychophysiology at the

University of North Carolina, and her colleague Sara Algoe, teaches soldiers how to amplify positive emotions and how to recognize when negative ones, such as sadness and anger, are out of proportion to the reality of the threat they face.

Family fitness, too, affects work performance, and cell phones, email, Facebook, and Skype allow even soldiers on combat duty, or expats on assignment, to remain intimately involved with their families. A course created by John and Julie Gottman, eminent psychologists specializing in marriage, focuses on building a variety of relationship skills—including fostering trust, constructively managing conflict, creating shared meaning, and recovering from betrayal.

The social fitness module, developed by John Cacioppo, a professor of psychology at the University of Chicago and an expert on loneliness, teaches empathy to soldiers by explaining mirror neurons in the brain. When you see another person in pain, your brain activity is similar but not identical to what it is when you yourself are in pain. The module then asks soldiers to practice identifying emotions in others, with an emphasis on racial and cultural diversity. This is at the heart of developing emotional intelligence—and diversity in the U.S. Army is a way of life, not just a political slogan.

The spiritual fitness module, created by Kenneth Pargament, a professor of psychology at Bowling Green State University, and Colonel Patrick Sweeney, a professor of behavioral sciences and leadership at West Point, takes soldiers through the process of building a "spiritual core" with self-awareness, a sense of agency, self-regulation, self-motivation, and social awareness. "Spiritual" in CSF refers not to religion but to belonging to and serving something larger than the self.

The mandatory module, on post-traumatic growth, is highly relevant for business executives facing failure. Created by Richard Tedeschi, a professor of psychology at the University of North Carolina at Charlotte, and the Harvard psychologist Richard McNally, it begins with the ancient wisdom that personal transformation comes from a renewed appreciation of being alive, enhanced personal strength, acting on new possibilities, improved relationships, or spiritual deepening. The module interactively teaches soldiers about five elements known to contribute to post-traumatic growth:

1. Understanding the response to trauma (read "failure"), which includes shattered beliefs about the self, others, and the future. This is a normal response, not a symptom of PTSD or a character defect.

2. Reducing anxiety through techniques for controlling intrusive thoughts and images.

3. Engaging in constructive self-disclosure. Bottling up trauma can lead to a worsening of physical and psychological symptoms, so soldiers are encouraged to tell their stories.

4. Creating a narrative in which the trauma is seen as a fork in the road that enhances the appreciation of paradox—loss and gain, grief and gratitude, vulnerability and strength. A manager might compare this to what the leadership studies pioneer Warren Bennis called "crucibles of leadership." The narrative specifies what personal strengths were called upon, how some relationships improved, how spiritual life strengthened, how life itself was better appreciated, or what new doors opened.

5. Articulating life principles. These encompass new ways to be altruistic, crafting a new identity, and taking seriously the idea of the Greek hero who returns from Hades to tell the world an important truth about how to live.

Master Resilience Training

The third and most important component of Comprehensive Soldier Fitness is the master resilience training for drill sergeants and other leaders, given at the University of Pennsylvania; at Victory University, in Memphis, Tennessee; at Fort Jackson, South Carolina; and by mobile teams working with troops in Germany and Korea. MRT can be seen as management training—teaching leaders how to embrace resilience and then pass on the knowledge. The content of MRT divides into three parts—building mental toughness, building signature strengths, and building strong relationships. All three are patterned after the Penn Resiliency Program and use plenary lectures, breakout sessions that include role playing, worksheets, and small-group discussion.

Building mental toughness

This segment of MRT is similar in theme to the online emotional fitness course for individual soldiers. It starts with Albert Ellis's ABCD model: C (emotional consequences) stem not directly from A (adversity) but from B (one's beliefs about adversity). The sergeants work through a series of A's (falling out of a three-mile run, for example) and learn to separate B's—heat-of-the-moment thoughts about the situation ("I'm a failure")—from C's, the emotions generated by those thoughts (such as feeling down for the rest of the day and thus performing poorly in the next training exercise). They then learn D—how to quickly and effectively dispel unrealistic beliefs about adversity.

Next we focus on thinking traps, such as overgeneralizing or judging a person's worth or ability on the basis of a single action. We illustrate this as follows: "A soldier in your unit struggles to keep up during physical training and is dragging the rest of the day. His uniform looks sloppy, and he makes a couple of mistakes during artillery practice. It might be natural to think that he lacks the stuff of a soldier. But what effect does that have on both the thinker and the other soldier?" We also discuss "icebergs"—deeply held beliefs such as "Asking for help is a sign of weakness"—and teach a technique for identifying and eliminating those that cause out-of-kilter emotional reactions: Does the iceberg remain meaningful? Is it accurate in the given situation? Is it overly rigid? Is it useful?

Finally, we deal with how to minimize catastrophic thinking by considering worst-case, best-case, and most likely outcomes. For example, a sergeant receives a negative performance evaluation from his commanding officer. He thinks, "I won't be recommended for promotion, and I don't have what it takes to stay in the army." That's the worst case. Now let's put it in perspective. What's the best case? "The negative report was a mistake." And what's the most likely case? "I will receive a corrective action plan from my counselor, and I will follow it. I'll be frustrated, and my squad leader will be disappointed."

Building signature strengths

The second part of the training begins with a test similar to the GAT—Peterson's Values in Action signature strengths survey, which is taken online and produces a ranked list of the test taker's top 24 character strengths. (See the sidebar "What Are Your

What Are Your Strengths?

The Values in Action signature strengths survey measures 24 positive character traits, among them curiosity, creativity, bravery, persistence, integrity, fairness, leadership, and self-regulation. Participants rank statements on a scale from "very much like me" to "very much unlike me" to determine the areas in which they shine. Here is a sampling:

- I find the world a very interesting place.
- I always identify the reasons for my actions.
- I never quit a task before it is done.
- Being able to come up with new and different ideas is one of my strong points.
- I have taken frequent stands in the face of strong opposition.
- I am always willing to take risks to establish a relationship.
- I always admit when I am wrong.
- In a group, I try to make sure everyone feels included.
- I always look on the bright side.
- I want to fully participate in life, not just view it from the sidelines.

Strengths?") Small groups discuss these questions: What did you learn about yourself from the survey? Which strengths have you developed through your military service? How do your strengths contribute to your completing a mission and reaching your goals? What are the shadow sides of your strengths, and how can you minimize them? Then the sergeants are put on teams and told to tackle a mission using the team members' character-strength profiles. Finally, the sergeants write their own "strengths in challenges" stories. One sergeant described how he used his strengths of love, wisdom, and gratitude to help a soldier who was acting out and stirring up conflict. The sergeant discovered that the soldier felt consumed by anger at his wife, and the anger spilled over to his unit. The sergeant used his wisdom to help the soldier understand the wife's perspective and worked with him to write a letter in which the soldier described the gratitude he felt because his wife had handled so much on her own during his three deployments.

Building strong relationships

The third part of MRT focuses on practical tools for positive communication. We draw on the work of Shelly Gable, a psychology professor at UC Santa Barbara, which shows that when an individual responds actively and constructively (as opposed to passively and destructively) to someone who is sharing a positive experience, love and friendship increase. (See the sidebar "Four Ways to Respond.") The sergeants complete a worksheet about how they typically respond and identify factors that may get in the way of active and constructive responses (such as being tired or overly focused on themselves). Next we teach the work of the Stanford psychology professor Carol Dweck on effective praise. When, for example, a sergeant mentions specifics (as opposed to saying something general like "Good job!"), his soldiers know that their leader was paying attention and that the praise is authentic. We also teach assertive communication, distinguishing it from passive or aggressive communication. What is the language, voice tone, body language, and pace of each of the three styles, and what messages do they convey?

Enhancing mental toughness, highlighting and honing strengths, and fostering strong relationships are core competen-

> ## Four Ways to Respond
>
> In master resilience training we explain and demonstrate the four styles of responding: *active constructive* (authentic, enthusiastic support), *passive constructive* (laconic support), *passive destructive* (ignoring the event), and *active destructive* (pointing out negative aspects of the event).
>
> Here's an example: Private Johnson tells Private Gonzales, "Hey, I just got a promotion."
>
> - *Active constructive.* "That's great. What are your new duties? When do you start? What did the captain say about why you deserved it?"
>
> - *Passive constructive.* "That's nice."
>
> - *Passive destructive.* "I got a funny email from my son. Listen to this..."
>
> - *Active destructive.* "You know there's no extra pay, and it will eat up a lot of your R&R time."

cies for any successful manager. Leadership development programs often touch on these skills, but the MRT program brings them together in systematic form to ensure that even in the face of terrible failures—those that cost lives—army sergeants know how to help the men and women under their command flourish rather than flounder. Managers can change the culture of their organizations to focus on the positive instead of the negative and, in doing so, turn pessimistic, helpless Walters into optimistic, can-do Douglases. Frankly, we were nervous that these hard-boiled soldiers would find resilience training "girly" or "touchy-feely" or "psychobabble." They did not; in fact, they gave the course an average rating of 4.9 out of 5.0. A large number of them say it's the best course they've ever had in the army.

We believe that MRT will build a better army. Our hypothesis is being tested in a large-scale study under the command of Lieutenant Colonel Sharon McBride and Captain Paul Lester. As the program rolls out, they are comparing the performance of soldiers who have been taught resilience by their sergeants with that of soldiers who haven't. When they are finished, we will know conclusively whether resilience training and positive psychology can make adults in a large organization more effective, as they have done for younger people in schools.

Originally published in April 2011. Reprint R1104H

QUICK READ

Do You Know When to Quit?

by André Spicer

When Vontae Davis walked off the field at halftime, the Buffalo Bills were down 28–6 to the Los Angeles Chargers. But instead of huddling with teammates, the Bills cornerback quit football entirely, right then and there. Later that evening, Davis announced his retirement on social media, saying, "Today on the field, reality hit me hard and fast: I shouldn't be out there anymore." Many were outraged, including Bills linebacker Lorenzo Alexander: "It's just completely disrespectful to his teammates." But some disagreed, saying Davis was "a goddamn working class hero."[1]

While unorthodox, Davis's abrupt mid-game retirement sparked strong emotions for a variety of reasons, including a question many of us ask: "How long should I stick with something?" Fortunately, we don't have to rely on NFL commentators to find answers to this question.

Perseverance has received lots of support in recent years from a variety of schools of research. One is from psychologists studying grit. They have found that the capacity to stick to a task—particularly when faced with difficulties—is a crucial factor in explaining the success of everyone, from kids in the national spelling bee to recruits at West Point to Ivy League undergraduates.

Then there's the idea that persevering in the face of adversity can prompt learning and improvements of skills. Carol Dweck's work on growth mindsets has found that those who treat challenges and limitations as an opportunity to develop and learn tend to perform better in the long term. They persist when they face challenges, and the reward is a deeper and wider skill set.

A final benefit of perseverance is that we don't know when our luck will turn. A study of the careers of nearly 29,000 artists, filmmakers, and scientists found that most of them had a hot streak in their careers when their work received wide acclaim.[2] These hot streaks happened at a random time in their careers, however. They weren't related to age, experience, or even being more productive. They just happened. This suggests that if you're thinking about quitting, you should remember that a hot streak could be just around the corner.

Other research challenges these findings, however. One meta-analysis of studies of over 66,000 people found that there was actually a weak link between grit and performance.[3] And a study of over 5,600 students taking scholastic aptitude tests found that there was no link between growth mindsets and scores on the test.[4] People with growth mindsets were not more likely to improve if they took the test again, nor were they more likely to even try to take the test again. And the research on the artists' hot streaks? It turns out most people had only one; second acts were comparatively rare, particularly for filmmakers. So if you've already enjoyed a streak of success, the odds are against you enjoying another one.

Idea in Brief

The Problem

Perseverance is often celebrated, but it can have downsides. People who persist with unachievable goals may experience stress, depression, and physical health issues. They may also waste time on unproductive tasks and miss out on better opportunities.

The Solution

The benefits and costs of perseverance should be evaluated carefully. Weigh the potential to continue learning and developing incrementally against the costs, dangers, and myopia that can come with grit.

The Benefits

Quitting can lead to better mental and physical health, reduced stress, and more satisfaction. You can then explore new opportunities and focus on rewarding and achievable goals to potentially lead a more fulfilling life.

In fact, there's a large body of work showing that perseverance may have a harmful downside. Not giving up can mean people persist even when they have nothing to gain. In one study, people working on an online platform were given a very boring task.[5] The researchers found those who said they were very persistent continued to do the task despite the fact it was boring and there was little to be gained in terms of monetary reward. So while it might be valuable to persist with worthwhile and rewarding tasks, people who don't quit often continue with worthless tasks that are both uninteresting and unrewarding, ultimately wasting their time and talents.

Remaining fixated on long-cherished goals can also mean people ignore better alternatives. Baseball players on minor league teams are a great example of this. These players often receive low pay and have little job security but live in the hope of

How Good Are You at Quitting?

For each question, give yourself a score from 1 (almost never true) to 5 (almost always true).

If I had to stop pursuing an important goal in my life...

1. It's easy for me to reduce my effort toward the goal.
2. I find it easy to stop trying to achieve the goal.
3. I am not committed to the goal for a long time; I can let it go.
4. It's easy for me to stop thinking about the goal and let it go.
5. I think about other new goals to pursue.
6. I seek other meaningful goals.
7. I convince myself that I have other meaningful goals to pursue.
8. I tell myself that I have a number of other new goals to draw on.
9. I start working on other new goals.
10. I put effort toward other meaningful goals.

Once you've completed the test, add up your score of questions 1 to 4. This will give you a sense of how good you are at disengaging from an existing goal. The average score is about 10. If you scored 13 or more, then you are very good at disengaging from old goals. If you scored 7 or less, then you are very bad at disengaging from old goals.

Now add up your scores for questions 5 to 10. That will give you a sense of how good you are at setting new goals. The average is 21 to 22. If you scored 26 or more, then you are very good at setting new goals. If you scored 17 or less, then you are very bad at setting new goals.

Note

a. Carsten Wrosch, Michael F. Scheier, and Gregory E. Miller, "Goal Adjustment Capacities, Subjective Well-Being, and Physical Health," *Social and Personality Psychology Compass* 7, no. 12 (2013): 847–860, https://pmc.ncbi.nlm.nih.gov/articles/PMC4145404/.

being spotted and making it into the major league. Only about 11% of players will make that transition. The other 89% are left languishing for years. If they stopped playing baseball, they would be more likely to find alternative employment that is more secure, pays more, and has a more defined career path. In short, by remaining under the spell of their dream, they are unable to explore other options that might be more lucrative.

Being unwilling to let go can lead to perpetual dissatisfaction—even when people end up getting what they thought they wanted. This was nicely illustrated in a study of graduating college students searching for a job.[6] The researchers found that students who had a tendency to "maximize" their options and were fixated on achieving the best possible job did end up getting 20% more in terms of salary. However, they were generally more dissatisfied with the job they got, and they found the process of getting the job more painful.

An unwillingness to quit can be more than just unrewarding. In some situations, it can become downright dangerous. This happens when people's persistence leads them to continue with, or even double down on, losing courses of action. One study found that people who were particularly gritty were less likely to give up when they were failing.[7] These same people were more likely to be willing to suffer monetary losses just so they could continue doing a task. Another study of would-be inventors found that over half would continue with their invention even after receiving reliable advice that it was fatally flawed, sinking more money into the project in the process.[8] The lesson: People who tend to be tenacious are also those who get trapped into losing courses of action.

Being unable to let go of cherished but unachievable goals can also be bad for your mental and physical health.[9] People who struggle to disengage with impossible goals tend to feel more stress, show more symptoms of depression, be plagued by intrusive thoughts, and find it difficult to sleep. They have higher rates of eczema, headaches, and digestion issues. Being fixated on unachievable goals is also related to high levels of cortisol (which over time is linked with things like weight gain, high blood pressure, negative mood, and sleeping problems) and higher levels of C-reactive protein (which is linked with inflammation in the body).

So when you ask yourself whether to stick with a task or goal or to let it go, weigh the potential to continue learning and developing incrementally against the costs, dangers, and myopia that can come with stubborn perseverance.

Adapted from "When to Stick with Something—and When to Quit" on hbr.org, September 28, 2018. Reprint H04K7S

5

Beating Burnout

by Monique Valcour

Heavy workloads and deadline pressures are a fact of managerial life. Who doesn't feel overwhelmed or stretched thin sometimes? But when relentless work stress pushes you into the debilitating state we call burnout, it is a serious problem, affecting not just your own performance and well-being, both on the job and off, but also that of your team and your organization.

Hard data on the prevalence of burnout is elusive since it's not yet a clinical term separate from stress. Some researchers say that as few as 7% of professionals have been seriously impacted by burnout. But others have documented rates as high as 50% among medical residents and 85% among financial professionals. A 2013 ComPsych survey of more than 5,100 North American workers found that 62% felt high levels of stress, loss of control, and extreme fatigue. Research has also linked burnout to many negative physical and mental health outcomes, including coronary artery disease, hypertension, sleep disturbances, depression, and anxiety, as well as to increased alcohol and drug use. Moreover, burnout has been shown to produce feelings of futility and alienation, undermine the quality of relationships, and diminish long-term career prospects.

Consider the case of Barbara (last name withheld), the CEO of a PR firm that serves technology industry clients. During the 2001 collapse of the dot-com bubble, the challenge of keeping her business afloat added extra stress to an already intense workload. Focused on this "unrelenting hustle," she neglected her health, lost perspective, and began to doubt her own abilities. Cheryl (not her real name), a partner in the Philadelphia office of a global law firm, hit the same sort of wall after she agreed to take on multiple leadership roles there in addition to managing her full-time legal practice. "I felt like my body was running on adrenaline—trying to do a marathon at a sprint pace—all the time," she recalls. And yet she couldn't step back mentally from work. Another executive I know—let's call him Ari—felt trapped in his role as a consultant at a boutique firm. Toxic internal dynamics and client relationship practices that clashed with his values had eroded his sense of self to the point where he didn't know how to go on—or get out.

Over the past 15 years as a coach, researcher, and educator, I've helped thousands of clients, students, and executive-development program participants in similar predicaments learn to manage the stress that can cause burnout and to ultimately achieve more-sustainable career success. The process involves noticing and acknowledging the symptoms, examining the underlying causes, and developing preventive strategies to counteract your particular pattern of burnout.

Three Components

Thanks to the pioneering research of psychologist Christina Maslach and several collaborators, we know that burnout is a three-component syndrome that arises in response to chronic

Idea in Brief

The Problem

Burnout is a serious issue affecting individual performance, well-being, and organizational health. It manifests through exhaustion, cynicism, and inefficacy, leading to negative physical and mental health outcomes. Burnout is prevalent across various professions, with significant percentages of workers experiencing high levels of stress, loss of control, and extreme fatigue.

The Solution

To combat burnout, individuals should prioritize self-care, shift their perspective, reduce exposure to job stressors, and seek out connections. Strategies include good sleep habits, nutrition, exercise, social connections, meditating, and journaling. Altering your mindset, delegating tasks, and building supportive relationships can help lessen the effects of burnout.

The Benefits

Implementing these strategies can lead to a more sustainable career and a happier, healthier life. By understanding and addressing the symptoms and causes of burnout, you can recover and prevent future occurrences, ultimately enhancing your overall well-being and productivity.

---

stressors on the job. Let's examine each symptom—exhaustion, cynicism, and inefficacy—in turn.

Exhaustion is the central symptom of burnout. It comprises profound physical, cognitive, and emotional fatigue that undermines people's ability to work effectively and feel positive about what they're doing. This can stem from the demands of an always-on, 24/7 organizational culture, intense time pressure, or simply having too much to do, especially when you lack control over your work, dislike it, or don't have the necessary skills to accomplish it. In a state of exhaustion, you find that you're unable to concentrate or see the big picture; even routine and previously enjoyable tasks seem arduous, and it becomes difficult to drag yourself both into and out of the office. This is how burnout started for Cheryl. Her fuel tank was low, and it wasn't being adequately replenished.

Cynicism, also called depersonalization, represents an erosion of engagement. It is essentially a way of distancing yourself psychologically from your work. Instead of feeling invested in your assignments, projects, colleagues, customers, and other collaborators, you feel detached, negative, even callous. Cynicism can be the result of work overload, but it is also likely to occur in the presence of high conflict, unfairness, and lack of participation in decision-making. For example, after ignoring repeated directives to push solutions that didn't solve clients' problems, Ari realized that the constant battle with his bosses was affecting his own behavior. "I was talking trash and shading the truth more often than I was being respectful and honest," he explains. Persistent cynicism is a signal that you have lost your connection to, enjoyment of, and pride in your work.

Inefficacy refers to feelings of incompetence and a lack of achievement and productivity. People with this symptom of burnout feel their skills slipping and worry that they won't be able to succeed in certain situations or accomplish certain tasks. It often develops in tandem with exhaustion and cynicism because people can't perform at their peak when they're out of fuel and have lost their connection to work. For example, although Barbara was a seasoned PR professional, the stress of the dot-com crisis and her resulting fatigue caused her to question her ability to serve clients and keep the business thriving. But burnout can also start with inefficacy if you lack the resources and support to do your job well, including adequate time, information, clear expectations, autonomy, and good relationships with those whose involvement you need to succeed. The absence of feedback and meaningful recognition, which leaves you wondering about the quality of your work and feeling that it's unappreciated, can also activate this component. This was the situation for Ari, who felt that he was forced to function at a subpar level because his organization didn't care enough to support good performance.

While each component is correlated with the other two and one often leads to another, individuals also have distinct burnout profiles. Michael Leiter, a longtime collaborator with Maslach, is examining this in his current research. He has found, for example, that some people are mainly exhausted but haven't yet developed cynicism or begun to doubt their performance. Others are primarily cynical or suffer most from feelings of reduced efficacy. People can also be high on two components and low on one. Although most of the prevention and recovery strategies we'll discuss are designed to address all three symptoms, it's a good idea to diagnose your specific burnout profile so that you know where you need the most help.

Recovery and Prevention

Situational factors are the biggest contributors to burnout, so changes at the job, team, or organizational level are often required to address all the underlying issues. However, there are steps you can take on your own once you're aware of the symptoms and of what might be causing them. Here are some strategies I have found to be successful with my clients.

Prioritize self-care

It's essential to replenish your physical and emotional energy, along with your capacity to focus, by prioritizing good sleep habits, nutrition, exercise, social connection, and practices that promote equanimity and well-being, like meditating, journaling, and enjoying nature. If you're having troubling squeezing such activities into your packed schedule, give yourself a week to assess exactly how you're spending your time. (You can do this on paper, in a spreadsheet, or on one of the many relevant apps now available.) For each block of time, record what you're doing, whom you're with, how you feel (for example, on a scale of 1 to 10, where 1 equals angry or drained and 10 is joyful or energized), and how valuable the activity is. This will help you find opportunities to limit your exposure to tasks, people, and situations that aren't essential and put you in a negative mood; increase your investment in those that boost your energy; and make space for restful, positive time away from work.

Barbara says she bounced back from her bout of burnout by "learning to do things that fill me up." Nowadays, when she notices that she's feeling overly tired or starting to doubt herself, she changes her behavior immediately, making use of flexible work options, hosting walking meetings to get out of the office, and setting limits on the amount of time she spends reading emails and taking calls from colleagues and clients.

After her crisis, Cheryl also became much more intentional about her time off. "I find that going away, getting a change of scenery, and 'taking it down a notch' allows my body and mind to rejuvenate," she says. "And my creativity benefits: I have more 'aha' moments, and I'm better able to connect the dots."

Shift your perspective

While rest, relaxation, and replenishment can ease exhaustion, curb cynicism, and enhance efficacy, they don't fully address the root causes of burnout. Back at the office, you may still face the same impossible workload, untenable conflicts, or paltry

Help Prevent Burnout on Your Team

Burnout is rarely an individual phenomenon; fixing and preventing it requires leadership. You can help your team thrive by implementing the following advice.

Watch for Warning Signs

- The signs of burnout are obvious in some people but subtle in others. Keep an eye out for tiredness, lack of focus, depressed mood, hostility, and expressions of hopelessness.
- Regularly check in with team members to gauge their physical, cognitive, and emotional energy levels.

Set Limits on Workloads

- Talk to your team about its collective capacity, and ensure that assignments and deadlines don't exceed it.
- Shield your team from external pressures, including unreasonable or unclear client and management demands.

Insist on Renewal

- Communicate that optimal performance depends on rest and renewal. Encourage people to set sensible limits on work hours.
- Set an example by keeping reasonable hours yourself.
- Make sure your team members take their full vacation time.

Boost Control

- Clarify expectations; grant flexibility on where, when, and how people get work done.
- Advocate for the resources your team needs to perform.
- Create uninterrupted time for people to make progress on important tasks.

(continued)

> **Help Prevent Burnout on Your Team** *(continued)*
>
> **Make Recognition Meaningful**
> - Regularly highlight wins and successes, even small ones.
> - Recognize and reward people for helping others.
> - Note the positive impact of your team's work on others.
>
> **Emphasize Learning**
> - Routinely ask team members about their development goals and what resources are required to achieve them.
> - Share what you're learning and how you're doing it.
>
> **Facilitate Mutual Support**
> - Talk regularly about progress toward team goals.
> - At team meetings, ask what assistance people need and can offer one another.
> - Be open about asking for and giving support.
>
> **Build Community**
> - Don't tolerate incivility on your team. Set an example for respectful, compassionate behavior toward others.
> - Encourage people to share what's happening in their lives outside of work.

resources. So now you must take a close look at your mindset and assumptions. What aspects of your situation are truly fixed, and which can you change? Altering your perspective can buffer the negative impact of even the inflexible aspects. If exhaustion is a key problem, ask yourself which tasks—including critical ones—you could delegate to free up meaningful time and energy for other important work. Are there ways to reshape your job in order to gain more control or to focus on the most fulfilling tasks? If cynicism is a major issue, can you shield yourself from the parts of the organization that frustrate you, while reengaging in your specific role and the whole enterprise? Or could you build some positive, supportive relationships to counteract the ones that drain you? And if you're feeling ineffective, what assistance or development might you seek out? If recognition is lacking, could you engage in some personal branding to showcase your work?

Cheryl worked with an executive coach to evaluate and reset her priorities. "I work in a competitive field and I'm a competitive person, which can skew the way you see reality," she explains. "In the past I didn't dare say no to leadership opportunities because I was afraid that if I did, everything might disappear." She says she's now replaced that "scarcity" mentality with one that instead presumes abundance. "Now if I feel overextended, I'll ask myself, Is there a way to inject joy back into this role, or is it time to give it up? And I understand that when I want to take something on, I need to decide what to give up to make space."

Ari did the same sort of deep thinking. Although he had previously felt tethered to his job—the firm was prestigious, the pay was good—he realized that values and ethics meant more to him than any perk, so he eventually quit and started his own business. "After I pushed back a couple of times and said that what we were recommending wasn't right for the clients, my boss cranked up the pressure on me and assigned me to only the most difficult clients. At one point I said to my wife, 'It might be good if I got hit by a bus. I don't want to die, but I'd like to be injured enough that I'd have to stop working for a while.' She said, 'That's it; you're getting out of there.'" He took a few months to line up some independent consulting assignments and then made the move.

Reduce exposure to job stressors

You'll also need to target high-value activities and relationships that still trigger unhealthy stress. This involves resetting the expectations of colleagues, clients, and even family members for what and how much you're willing to take on, as well as ground rules for working together. You may get pushback. But doubters must know that you're making these changes to improve your long-term productivity and protect your health.

Barbara, for example, is keenly aware of the aspects of PR work that put people in her field at risk of burnout, so now she actively manages them. "There's constant pressure, from both clients and the media," she explains. "But a lot of times, what clients label a crisis is not actually one. Part of the job is helping them put things in perspective. And being a good service professional doesn't mean you have to be a servant. You shouldn't be emailing at 11 at night on a regular basis."

Cheryl, too, says she's learned "not to get carried along in the current" of overwhelming demands. She adds, "You have to know when saying no is the right answer. And it takes courage and conviction to stick to your guns and not feel guilty." If you find that there are few or no opportunities to shift things in a more positive direction, you might want to contemplate a bigger change, as Ari did.

Seek out connections

The best antidote to burnout, particularly when it's driven by cynicism and inefficacy, is seeking out rich interpersonal interactions and continual personal and professional development.

Find coaches and mentors who can help you identify and activate positive relationships and learning opportunities. Volunteering to advise others is another particularly effective way of breaking out of a negative cycle.

Given the influence of situational factors on burnout, it's likely that others in your organization are suffering too. If you band together to offer mutual support, identify problems, and brainstorm and advocate for solutions, you will all increase your sense of control and connection. Barbara participates in a CEO mentoring and advisory program called Vistage. "We're a small group of CEOs in noncompetitive businesses, so we can share ideas," she explains. "We spend one day per month together, have great speakers, and serve as advisory boards for each other." Ari, now a successful solo entrepreneur, has built a network of technical partners who share the same vision, collaborate, and funnel work to one another. He says that running a "client centered" business he believes in and working with people he respects have boosted his engagement tremendously.

. . .

Burnout can often feel insurmountable. But the sense of being overwhelmed is a signal, not a long-term sentence. By understanding the symptoms and causes and implementing these four strategies, you can recover and build a road map for prevention. Your brutal experience can serve as a turning point that launches you into a more sustainable career and a happier, healthier life.

Originally published in November 2016. Reprint R1611H

QUICK READ

Burnout Is About Your Workplace, Not Your People

by Jennifer Moss

We tend to think of burnout as an individual problem, solvable by learning to say no, doing more yoga, employing better breathing techniques, practicing resilience—the self-help list goes on. But evidence is mounting that applying personal, Band-Aid solutions to an epic and rapidly evolving workplace phenomenon may be more harmful than helpful. With "burnout" now officially recognized by the World Health Organization (WHO), the responsibility for managing it has shifted away from the individual and toward the organization. Leaders take note: It's now on *you* to build a burnout strategy.

The term "burnout" originated in the 1970s, and for the past 50 years, the medical community has argued about how to define it. The debate has been contentious and confusing. In 2019, the WHO included burnout in its International Classification of Diseases (ICD-11), and immediately the public assumed that burnout would now be considered a medical condition. Within weeks, the WHO then put out an urgent clarification stating, "Burn-out is included in the 11th Revision of the International Classification of Diseases (ICD-11) as an occupational phenomenon, *not* a medical condition . . . reasons for which people contact health services but that are not classed as illnesses or health conditions."

Most organizations still have no idea what to do about burnout. Since it was explicitly not classified as a medical condition, burnout is less about liability for employers and more about the impact on employee well-being and the massive associated costs.

The Emotional and Financial Toll

When Stanford researchers looked into how workplace stress affects health costs and mortality in the United States, they found that it led to spending of nearly $190 billion—roughly 8% of national health care outlays—and nearly 120,000 deaths each year.[1] Worldwide, 615 million suffer from depression and anxiety that, according to a WHO study, costs the global workforce an estimated $1 trillion in lost productivity each year.[2] Passion-driven and caregiving people such as doctors and nurses are some of the most susceptible to burnout, and the consequences can mean life or death; suicide rates among caregivers are dramatically higher than those of the general public—40% higher for men and 130% higher for women.[3]

If those statistics aren't scary enough, consider the fact that companies without systems to support the well-being of their employees have higher turnover, lower productivity, and higher health care costs, according to the American Psychological Association (APA).[4] In high-pressure firms, health care costs are

Idea in Brief

The Problem
Burnout is often misunderstood as an individual issue, but it is actually a workplace phenomenon. Burnout results from factors like unfair treatment, unmanageable workload, lack of role clarity, poor communication, and unreasonable time pressure. These issues lead to significant emotional and financial tolls.

The Solution
To address burnout, leaders must create a safe and supportive work environment by addressing the root causes of burnout. They should ask employees what they need to thrive and implement small, targeted interventions. This includes better organizational hygiene, data-driven decision-making, and ensuring that wellness offerings are part of the overall well-being strategy.

The Benefits
By tackling burnout, companies can reduce health care costs, improve productivity, and retain talent. Employees will experience better mental health, increased job satisfaction, and a more positive work culture.

50% greater than at other organizations.[5] Workplace stress is estimated to cost the U.S. economy more than $500 billion, and, each year, 550 million workdays are lost due to stress on the job.[6] Another study by the APA claims that burned-out employees are 2.6 times as likely to be actively seeking a different job, 63% more likely to take a sick day, and 23% more likely to visit the emergency room.[7]

Obviously, this is a real problem. And it can feel like a Herculean task for leaders to tackle, perhaps because the concept seems too ambiguous or overwhelming. When experts still struggle to define burnout, how can we ask our managers to actually prevent it?

It's Not Me, It's You

According to the foremost expert on burnout, Christina Maslach, social psychologist and professor emerita of psychology at the University of California, Berkeley, we are attacking the problem from the wrong angle. She is one of three people responsible for the gold standard of measuring burnout—the eponymous Maslach Burnout Inventory (MBI)—and the coauthor of the Areas of Worklife Survey. Maslach worries about the WHO classification in the ICD-11. "Categorizing burnout as a disease was an attempt by the WHO to provide definitions for what is wrong with people, instead of what is wrong with companies," she explains. "When we just look at the person, what that means is, 'Hey, we've got to treat that person.' 'You can't work here because you're the problem.' 'We have to get rid of that person.' Then, it becomes that person's problem, not the responsibility of the organization that employs them."

To Maslach's point, a Gallup survey of 7,500 full-time employees found the top five reasons for burnout are:[8]

1. Unfair treatment at work

2. Unmanageable workload

3. Lack of role clarity

4. Lack of communication and support from their manager

5. Unreasonable time pressure

This list clearly demonstrates that the root causes of burnout do not really lie with the individual and that they can be averted—if only leadership started prevention strategies much further upstream.

In our interview, Maslach asked me to picture canaries in a coal mine. They are healthy birds, singing away as they make their way into the cave. But when they come out full of soot and disease, no longer singing, can you imagine us asking why the canaries made themselves sick? No, because the answer would be obvious: The *coal mine* is making the birds sick.

This visual struck me. Although developing emotional intelligence skills—like optimism, gratitude, and hope—can give people the rocket fuel they need to be successful, if an employee is dealing with burnout, we have to stop and ask ourselves why. We should never suggest that if they'd just practiced more grit or joined another yoga class or taken a mindfulness course, they would have avoided burnout. I have long been a proponent of empathy and optimism in leadership. I believe in practicing gratitude skills for a happier, higher-performing work and life experience. I endorse the idea of building resilience to better handle stress when it arises. But these skills are not the cure for burnout, nor are they the vaccine.

So, what is?

First, ask yourself as a leader, what is making my staff so unhealthy? Why does our work environment lack the conditions for them to flourish? How can I make it safe for them to work here every day? We have to dig into the data and ask our people what would make work better for them. More generally, we need to better understand what causes people to feel motivated in our organizations, and what causes them frustration.

Motivation-Hygiene Theory

Frederick Herzberg is known for his dual-factor, motivation-hygiene theory—essentially, what motivates us versus what basic needs must be met in order to maintain job satisfaction. Herzberg found that satisfaction and dissatisfaction are not on a continuum with one increasing as the other diminishes but are instead independent of each other. This means that managers need to recognize and attend to both equally.

Motivators are different from hygiene factors. Motivation factors include challenging work, recognition for one's achievements, responsibility, the opportunity to do something meaningful, involvement in decision-making, and a sense of importance to the organization. On the other hand, hygiene factors include salary, work conditions, company policy and administration, supervision, working relationships, status, and security.

Often, employees don't recognize when an organization has good hygiene, but bad hygiene can cause a major distraction. The latter can come down to seemingly innocuous issues, like having coffee in the break room one day and no coffee the next. People feel it. Burnout happens when these presupposed features in our day-to-day work lives are missing or taken away.

Maslach has affectionately named this feeling "pebbles." She describes them as the tiny, incremental, irritating, and painful things at work that can wear you down. Through my work, I've seen this in action. Consider this example: The music faculty chairs at a university where I worked decided to put their entire annual improvement budget toward building a soundproof studio. They were certain the rest of the group would be thrilled. They were wrong. In reality, staff just wanted new music stands at a cost of $300. The existing ones were imbalanced or broken, and students would often find their sheet music on the floor when practicing. The ribbon-cutting event for the studio was lackluster, and engagement was low. Some faculty didn't even show up. The leadership expressed frustration with the lack of gratitude. Neither group shared their dissatisfaction with the other, and over the course of the following year, that seed of anger grew. The nontenured high-performers sought out new opportunities, and the faculty lost talent. If staff had been given a say in how the budget was allocated, the team might still be intact for just $300.

Maslach told me a story of a CEO who decided to put a volleyball court on the roof of his office building. Employees would look up at it and see how few people were using it. It would make them cynical because that money could have been going to so many other things. Maslach said, "They would think, *If only I had some of that budget, I could fix [insert problem to be solved here].*"

Leaders could save themselves a huge amount of employee stress and subsequent burnout if they were just better at asking people what they need.

Ask Better Questions

When investing in burnout prevention strategies, it's best to narrow down the efforts to small, micro-pilots, which means a lower budget and less risk. I suggest starting with one or two departments or teams and asking one simple question: "If we had this much budget and could spend it on X many items in our department, what would be the first priority?" Have the team vote anonymously and then share the data with everyone. Discuss what was prioritized and why, and start working down the list. Employees may not have the perfect silver-bullet solution, but they can most certainly tell us what isn't working—and that is often the most invaluable data.

A larger pilot can start with some critical but some simple tactics. For example, take a referendum on some of the annual events. Ask your employees if they like the holiday party or the annual picnic. What would they keep? What would they change? Or is there something else that they would rather do with that money? Digital tools and simple surveys are easy to use and deploy—particularly if you ask a simple question. What's critical to making this tactic successful is how you use the data. Before engaging in a practice like this—or any employee survey, for that matter—decide what to do with the information. If you ask questions and don't bother with a reply, people begin to get wary and stop answering truthfully, or at all.

If sending out questions digitally doesn't feel right, start by walking around. Some of the best data-gathering comes from the MBWA style of leadership—management by wandering around. Maslach says she's witnessed hospital CEOs walking the floor only to realize why people keep asking for, say, a new printer. They see that because the existing one is always breaking down and never serviced, it rarely has paper. So when someone wants to print out something for a patient, they are forced to run down the hall and get somebody to help or to find a printer that works. It's hard for leadership to then ignore needs after witnessing them firsthand.

Organizations have a chance, right now, to fix this situation. Burnout is preventable. It requires good organizational hygiene, better data, asking more timely and relevant questions, smarter (more micro) budgeting, and ensuring that wellness offerings are included as part of your well-being strategy. Keep the yoga, the resilience training, and the mindfulness classes—they are all terrific tools for optimizing mental health and managing stress. But when it comes to employee burnout, remember, it's on *you* as a leader, not them.

Adapted from hbr.org, December 11, 2019. Reprint H05BI7

An Antidote to Incivility

by Christine Porath

When I was 22, I scored what I thought was my dream job. I moved from the snowy Midwest to sunny Florida with a group of fellow former college athletes to help a global athletic brand launch a sports academy. But within two years I and many of my peers had left our jobs.

We had fallen victim to a work culture rife with bullying, rudeness, and other incivility that was set by a dictatorial head of the organization and had trickled down through the ranks. Employees were at best disengaged; at worst they undertook acts of sabotage or released their frustration on family members and friends. By the time I left, many of us were husks of our former selves.

That experience was so formative that I decided to spend my professional life studying workplace incivility—and its costs and remedies. My research has shown that it is almost impossible to be untouched by incivility during one's career. Over the past 20 years I've polled thousands of workers and found that 98% have experienced uncivil behavior and 99% have witnessed it. In 2011 half said they were treated badly at least once a week—up from a quarter in 1998. Rude behavior ranged from outright nastiness and intentional undermining to ignoring people's opinions to checking email during meetings.

As I and my colleagues at the sports academy discovered, incivility in the workplace drags down performance and takes a personal toll. In laboratory settings I've found that simply observing it makes people far less likely to absorb information. Seeing or experiencing rude behavior impairs working (short-term) memory and thus cognitive ability. It has been shown to damage the immune system, put a strain on families, and produce other deleterious effects.

Unfortunately, people's resilience to incivility is partly out of their control. Research has shown that responses to threat, humiliation, loss, or defeat—all commonly associated with incivility—are significantly influenced by genetic makeup. Perhaps as a result, the most effective way to reduce the costs of incivility in the workplace is to build a culture that rejects it—to adopt "the no asshole rule," as Robert Sutton calls it in his bestselling book by that name. But very few organizations can comprehensively enforce this rule. So when individuals encounter incivility, what should they do?

My research has uncovered some tactics that anyone can use to minimize the effects of rudeness on performance and well-being. I wish I could have shared these with my younger self as she floundered in a hostile work environment many years ago.

The Usual Responses Often Fall Short

Many people decide to tackle incivility head-on—through either retaliation or direct discussion. Another common response is to try to work around the problem by avoiding the perpetrator as

Idea in Brief

The Problem

Incivility in the workplace, including bullying and rudeness, significantly impacts employee performance and well-being. Research shows that 98% of workers have experienced uncivil behavior, leading to disengagement, sabotage, and personal tolls such as impaired cognitive ability and weakened immune systems.

The Solution

To combat the effects of incivility or rudeness on your health, you should focus on thriving both cognitively and emotionally. The most effective remedy is to work holistically on your well-being rather than trying to change the perpetrator or the relationship. When you *do* choose confrontation, prepare for the conversation carefully.

The Benefits

By fostering a thriving mentality, you can become more resilient to incivility, achieve better health, and maintain an engaged and happy professional life.

much as possible. Although these approaches can help in certain situations, I don't usually advise people to take them. Avoidance often falls apart, because sometimes you have no choice but to collaborate with discourteous colleagues. Confrontation can make the dynamic worse. In my surveys I've found that more than 85% of people who chose to avoid or confront perpetrators were unsatisfied with how the situation ended or how they handled it, and those who attempted confrontation were no more satisfied than those who didn't respond. Relying on institutional remedies rarely works either—a mere 15% report being satisfied with how their employers handle incivility. In fairness, organizations often have no opportunity to act: More than half of survey respondents say they don't report rudeness, largely out of fear or a sense of helplessness.

A Holistic Approach

Just as medicine is shifting from a focus on fighting illness to one on promoting wellness, research in my field—organizational behavior—has begun to discover that working to improve your well-being in the office, rather than trying to change the offender or the corrosive working relationship, is the most effective remedy for incivility.

That's not to say you shouldn't report a rude or bullying colleague to HR, or try to manage conflict directly. But a more sustainable way to deal with bad behavior is to make yourself impervious to it—or at least a lot less vulnerable. To do that, it's helpful to look at what we know about *thriving*—the psychological state in which a sense of vitality and self-improvement fortifies people against the vicissitudes of life.

In my research I have found that thriving people are healthier, more resilient, and better able to focus on their work. They are buffered against distraction, stress, and negativity. In a study of six organizations across industries, employees characterized as high thrivers burned out less than half as often as their peers. They were 52% more confident in themselves and their ability to take control of a situation, and their performance suffered 34% less after an unpleasant incident.

If you're thriving, you're less likely to worry about a hit or take it as a personal affront, more immune to the waves of emotion that follow, and more focused on navigating toward your goal. Yet despite these obvious advantages, fewer than half the people I've surveyed focus on themselves and work to foster a thriving mentality after a brush with incivility. Rarely do they consider that the antidote might be totally disconnected from the incident at hand.

How can you help yourself thrive? I suggest a two-pronged approach: Take steps to thrive *cognitively*, which includes growth, momentum, and continual learning; and take steps to thrive *affectively*, by which I mean feeling healthy and experiencing passion and excitement at work and outside it. These two tactics are often mutually reinforcing—if you have energy, you're more likely to be motivated to learn, and a sense of growth fuels your vitality. But distinguishing between them can help people recognize in which area they may be lagging and take steps to bolster their defenses for the next hostile encounter.

Thrive Cognitively

If you've dealt with a rude colleague, you probably know how hard it can be to get over it. Perhaps no feeling is more difficult to overcome than a sense of injustice. Neuroscientists have shown that memories attached to strong emotions are easier to access and more likely to be replayed, and ruminating on an incident prevents you from putting it behind you. This can cause greater insecurity, lower self-esteem, and a heightened sense of helplessness.

I encourage people to shift their focus to cognitive growth instead. Your conscious brain can think about only so many things at once—far better that it keep busy building new neural connections and laying down new memories.

You can allow yourself to feel hurt or outraged—but for a limited time only. Tina Sung, a vice president at the nonprofit Partnership for Public Service, shared with me a saying that captures this advice: "You can visit Pity City, but you can't live there." I might add that Pity City is a good place to drop off your baggage.

Journaling and other rituals can help bring closure. As David Brooks documents in his new book, *The Road to Character*, Dwight D. Eisenhower often wrote furious invective in his journal to release negative emotions related to colleagues. He started the habit while working as an aide to the famously tyrannical General Douglas MacArthur.

Once your attention has shifted to more-productive avenues, several steps can help you focus on cognitive growth. First, identify areas for development and actively pursue learning opportunities in them. Teresa Amabile and Steven Kramer have shown that progress is a more powerful motivator in the workplace than even recognition or pay. It can be equally effective in helping employees bounce back from incivility. One young woman working in marketing told me, "A toxic environment was chipping away at my soul." She saw no quick or easy path out of her position, so she decided to pursue an MBA at night. Events along the way, such as achieving a great GMAT score, provided excitement and confidence. Although her future remained unclear, she became more resilient to her corrosive workplace.

It's worth noting that these development efforts need not be linked directly to your job. Taking on a new skill, hobby, or sport can have a similar effect. It's simply harder to be dragged down when you feel on the upswing.

Another way to promote cognitive growth is to work closely with a mentor. Mentors have a knack for helping their protégés thrive by challenging them and ensuring that they don't stagnate or get caught in an unproductive churn. For example, Lynne, a consultant working in an uncivil environment, built a close relationship with a mentor who urged her to steer clear of any unnecessary drama and focus on her own performance. When Lynne felt that she was slipping into rumination, recrimination, and anger, her mentor reminded her of the toll on her happiness and productivity and pointed her in more-fruitful directions. Following the advice, Lynne was able to dramatically improve her well-being—and her performance, which scored her a promotion.

Thrive Affectively

I find it useful to think of rude behavior in the workplace as an infectious pathogen, like a virus. Your defense against it depends in good measure on how well you are able to manage your energy. In fact, my research suggests that many of the factors that help prevent illness—such as good nutrition, sleep, and stress management—can also help ward off the noxious effects of incivility.

Sleep is particularly important: A lack of it increases your susceptibility to distraction and robs you of self-control; makes you feel less trusting, more hostile, more aggressive, and more threatened even by weak stimuli; and can induce unethical behavior. In short, sleep deprivation (usually defined as getting less than five hours a night) is a recipe for responding poorly to incivility and perhaps even damaging your career.

Exercise is another surefire way to protect yourself against the negative emotions, such as anger, fear, and sadness, that are typically brought on by rude behavior. It enhances both cognitive firepower and mood, distracts you from your concerns, reduces muscle tension, and improves resilience. It has been shown to slash symptoms of anxiety by more than 50%, and in one study it even proved to be more effective at treating depression than sertraline, a leading prescription for the illness. Those who exercise regularly are far less likely to sulk and better able to rebound in the wake of negative interactions.

> ## If You Choose Confrontation
>
> If you're thinking about confronting a colleague who's been rude, ask yourself three questions: (1) Do I feel safe talking with this person? (2) Was the behavior intentional? (3) Was it the only instance of such behavior by him or her?
>
> If you answered no to any of the questions, do not discuss the incident with the offender. Concentrate on your own effectiveness and, in future encounters, follow the acronym BIFF: Be *brief, informative, friendly,* and *firm*.
>
> But if you answered yes to all three questions, consider telling the offender how the behavior made you feel. Some things to keep in mind:
>
> *Prepare for the discussion.* Think about a good time and a safe environment in which you'll both be comfortable. Consider whether to invite other people to be witnesses or mediators.
>
> *Rehearse your ideas with someone who will give you honest feedback.* Ask that person to role-play the perpetrator, complete with temperament.

Maintaining your energy in other ways, such as eating healthfully, will also help put you in top form to respond smoothly to an uncivil encounter. When famished, most people tend to respond to frustration by lashing out.

But it's not just about caring for your body. Mindfulness—shifting your consciousness to process situations more slowly and thoughtfully and to respond with greater premeditation—can help you maintain your equilibrium in a difficult environment, as can finding a sense of purpose in your job. I and other researchers have discovered that when people are engaged in work they consider meaningful, they are more productive in uncivil teams than their colleagues are. Reminding yourself of

> *Be aware of your nonverbal communication.* This includes posture, facial expressions, gestures, tempo, timing, and especially tone of voice. People practice *what* they plan to say far more than *how* they will say it. But studies show that words convey far less meaning than does the way they're delivered.
>
> *Proceed with the goal of mutual gain.* During the discussion, focus on the issue (not the individual) and how the specific behavior harms performance.
>
> *Prepare for an emotional response.* If the perpetrator starts venting, try to tolerate it: It may lead to a more productive place. Use wording such as "I get that" or "I understand." Admitting blame when appropriate may also be helpful.
>
> *Be an active listener.* Paraphrase what you hear and repeat it. People gain credibility and are better liked when they ask humble questions.
>
> *Focus on establishing courteous norms for the future.* How will you interact so that neither of you suffers degraded performance moving forward?

nonmonetary attributes that attracted you to your work in the first place may foster gratitude and satisfaction.

Positive relationships within and outside the office also provide an emotional uplift that can directly counterbalance the effects of incivility. Research I conducted with Andrew Parker and Alexandra Gerbasi shows that across industries, organizations, and levels, "de-energizing," negative relationships have four to seven times as much impact on an employee's sense of thriving as do energizing, positive ones. In other words, you need a small group of energizers to offset the effects of each jerk. So think about the people in your life who make you laugh and who lift your spirits. Spend more time with them, and ask to be introduced to their friends.

Finally, in studies of MBAs, executive MBAs, and employees, I have found a consistently strong correlation between thriving outside work and resilience to incivility. In a study of people who experienced rudeness, those who flourished in nonwork activities reported 80% better health, 89% greater thriving at work, and 38% more satisfaction with how they had handled the encounter. Seeking leadership roles in the community—particularly if you have no immediate opportunity within your organization—bolsters both cognitive and affective thriving. One executive I interviewed decided to join the board of a nonprofit dedicated to improving the lives of patients with dup15q, a condition his daughter had inherited. He spearheaded fundraising efforts, helped build scientific interest, and stewarded the group's finances. These experiences and rewards, he told me, made him feel nearly bulletproof at work.

Incivility exacts a steep price. In extreme cases a job change or relocation may be needed to avoid burnout and to preserve your health and well-being. My research shows that for every eight people who report working in an uncivil environment, approximately one ultimately leaves as a direct result, and, looking back, I know I was right to exit the Florida sports academy. However, when I encounter rude behavior now, I'm better armed to offset its effects. Like everyone else, I'm still a work in progress, and my response is rarely perfect. But I can say with confidence that focusing on a sense of thriving has made me a more engaged, productive, and happy professional. You can be too.

Originally published in April 2016. Reprint R1604J

QUICK READ

Recognizing and Responding to Microaggressions at Work

by Ella F. Washington

We've all been in situations at work when someone says or does something that feels hostile or offensive to some aspect of our identity—and the person doesn't even realize it. These kinds of actions—insensitive statements, questions, or assumptions—are called "microaggressions," and they can target many aspects of who we are. For example, they could be related to someone's race, gender, sexuality, parental status, socioeconomic background, mental health, or any other aspect of our identity.

Most often, microaggressions are aimed at traditionally marginalized identity groups. Yet these hurtful actions can happen to anyone, of any background, at any professional level. A microaggression against a Black woman, for example, could be "You aren't like the other Black people I know" (indicating the person is different from the stereotypes of Black people), whereas one for a white male might be, "Oh, you don't ever have to worry about fitting in" (indicating that all white men are always comfortable and accepted). Essentially, microaggressions are based on a simple, damaging idea: "Because you are X, you probably are/are not or like/don't like Y."

One criticism of discourse about microaggressions is that our society has become hypersensitive and that casual remarks are now blown out of proportion. However, research is clear about the impact seemingly innocuous statements can have on one's physical and mental health, especially over the course of an entire career: increased rates of depression, prolonged stress and trauma, physical concerns like headaches, high blood pressure, and difficulties with sleep. Microaggressions can negatively impact careers as they are related to increased burnout and less job satisfaction and require significant cognitive and emotional resources to recover from them. One study found that 7 in 10 workers said they would be upset by a microaggression, and half said the action would make them consider leaving their job.

So the reality is that microaggressions are not so micro in terms of their impact. They should be taken seriously, because at their core they signal disrespect and reflect inequality.

To create inclusive, welcoming, and healthy workplaces, we must actively combat microaggressions. Doing so requires understanding how they show up and how to respond productively to them, whether they happen to us or to colleagues. Inclusive work environments are not just nice to have—they positively contribute to employee well-being and mental and physical health.[1]

Building inclusive workplaces requires candid, authentic conversations on tough subjects, like sexism, homophobia, and

Idea in Brief

The Problem

Microaggressions are hostile or offensive actions, often unintentional, that target aspects of one's identity, such as race or gender. These actions can lead to significant physical and mental health issues, including depression, stress, and burnout. Microaggressions signal disrespect and inequality, negatively impacting job satisfaction and increasing turnover.

The Solution

To combat microaggressions, individuals and organizations must increase awareness and respond productively. This involves understanding how microaggressions manifest, being intentional with language, and creating inclusive environments. Leaders should provide training, correct exclusionary behavior, and foster open, respectful dialogues. Individuals should pause, seek clarification, and apologize if they commit a microaggression.

The Benefits

When microaggressions are reduced and addressed, employees experience better mental health, increased job satisfaction, and a sense of belonging. Ultimately, creating inclusive environments where people can thrive enhances organizational success.

racism, and it's natural to worry that we may commit microaggressions in these kinds of conversations by saying the wrong thing. The more awareness we have about how microaggressions show up, the more we can work toward decreasing them in the workplace. Yet the reality is that we all make mistakes, so you should know what to do if you witness a microaggression or commit one.

As I share in my book *The Necessary Journey*, awareness is always the first step. Here are some ways to become more aware of microaggressions, interrupt them when we see them, and promote workplace cultures with fewer microaggressions.

Being More Aware of Microaggressions

There are many words and phrases in the English language that are rooted in systemically favoring dominant groups in society. Thus, many parts of our everyday speech have historical roots in racism, sexism, and other forms of discrimination. For example, the following terms you may casually hear in the workplace have hurtful connotations:

- "Blacklist" refers to a list of things that are seen negatively, juxtaposed against "whitelist," a list of things that are seen positively.

- "Man up" equates gender with strength or competence.

- "Peanut gallery" originated in the 1800s and referred to the sections of segregated theaters usually occupied by Black people.

These words and phrases can trigger thoughts of current and past discrimination. Taking time to be intentional with the language you use is a significant part of treating each other with respect. While it's unrealistic to know every cultural minefield that may exist in language, the goal is to be thoughtful about the origins of common phrases and, more importantly, to change your use of these terms if you become aware that they are problematic. For example, if you are looking to encourage someone, telling them to "rise to the moment" or "be brave" is a better way to communicate the sentiment than "man up." It takes work to unlearn the many fraught words and phrases in our cultural lexicon, but most people find it's not that difficult to do once they set their minds to actively being more inclusive.

Here are examples of a few types of microaggressions that you may hear within and outside the workplace:

- Race/Ethnicity
    - "I didn't realize you were Jewish—you don't look Jewish," signaling that a person of the Jewish heritage has a stereotypical look. (Of course, similar statements happen to people from many backgrounds.)
    - "I believe the most qualified person should get the job," signaling that someone is being given an unfair advantage because of their race.

- Citizenship
    - "Your English is so good. Where are your parents from?" signaling that people with English as a second language are generally less capable of speaking English.
    - "But where are you *really* from?" signaling that where someone grew up isn't their "true" origin. This microaggression often happens to people who are in ethnic and racial minorities, whom others assume are immigrants.

- Class
    - "How did you get into that school?" signaling that someone's background makes them an anomaly at a prestigious school.
    - "You don't seem like you grew up poor," signaling that someone from a particular socioeconomic background should look or behave a certain way.

- Mental health

    - "That's insane" or "That's crazy," using terminology related to a mental health condition to describe surprise or astonishment.

    - "You don't seem like you are depressed. Sometimes I get sad too," minimizing the experiences of people with mental illness.

    - "Don't mind my OCD!" using the acronym for obsessive compulsive disorder, a mental health condition where an individual is plagued by obsessive thoughts and fears that can lead to compulsions, to describe attention to detail, fastidiousness, or being organized.

- Gender

    - "Don't be so sensitive," signaling that someone, likely a woman, is being "too emotional" in a situation where a man would be more objective.

    - "Thanks, sweetheart" and similar comments often directed at women, which are often not appreciated or even offensive.

- Sexuality

    - "That's so gay" to mean something is bad or undesirable, signaling that being gay is associated with negative and undesirable characteristics.

    - "Do you have a wife/husband?" which assumes heteronormative culture and behaviors, versus more inclusive phrasing such as "Do you have a partner?"

- Parental status
  - "You don't have kids to pick up, so you can work later, right?" signaling that someone without children does not have a life outside of work.

In the workplace, microaggressions can happen in all types of conversations. For example, they may occur during hiring when someone is evaluating a candidate with a different demographic background than their own, during the performance evaluation process when someone is highlighting the positive or negative aspects of an employee, or in customer service when someone is interacting with customers who have a different first language than their own. We should all become more aware of microaggressions in general, but in professional environments, there should be a special level of attention to and care taken in the language we use.

Responding to Microaggressions

The more you increase your awareness of microaggressions, the more you will inevitably notice they are happening—and wonder how or if you should intercede. As with the advice given to victims of a microaggression, you have the option to respond in the moment or later on, or let it go.

There is no one right approach to dealing with microaggressions, but here are a few considerations for when you witness one.

1. What's the right moment to say something?

Consider the environment and be thoughtful about how to create a safe space for the conversation. Think about whether the conversation is best had in the moment (possibly in front of other people) or one-on-one.

In some situations, an in-the-moment approach may be sufficient. For example, if someone accidentally misgenders a colleague in a meeting, a leader could say, "Let's make sure we are using everyone's correct pronouns," and keep the meeting going. Doing this can make it less taboo to point out microaggressions and help to create a culture of positive in-the-moment correction when they happen.

But no one likes to be put on the spot, and conversations are much more likely to turn tense if your colleague feels like you are calling them out. So if you need to confront someone, try to "call them in" by creating a safe environment where you can engage the person in honest, authentic dialogue—without a client or other colleagues present—to say, "Hey, I know you didn't mean it this way, but let's not use language like . . ."

2. What's your relationship to the person who made the comment?

Do you have a personal relationship with the person who committed the microaggression? If so, you might be able to simply say, "Hey, you made a comment earlier that did not sit well with me."

However, if you do not have a personal relationship with the colleague, you may want to consider what you know about their personality (do they tend to be combative?) and history with uncomfortable conversations (are they generally approachable?). You may also need to bring in other colleagues they are closer with.

3. What's your personal awareness of the microaggression's subject?

Be honest about your level of familiarity with the subject at hand. For example, maybe you recognize that a comment is a racial microaggression, but you do not know the history or full implications of it. In that case, it's OK to talk to the person, but recognize you are not an authority on the topic and consider learning more first or talking to someone who has more familiarity with the topic.

Once you realize a microaggression has been committed and you decide to act, it's important to remind your friends or colleagues of the difference between *intent* and *impact*. While the speaker may not have intended the comment to be offensive, we must acknowledge the impact of our statements. Intent does not supersede or excuse actual impact. For example, you could say to the person, "I know you may have intended your statement to come off as _____, but the way I received it was _____." Sometimes simply highlighting the gap between intent and impact can be enlightening for the other person.

If You Realize You Have Committed a Microaggression

If someone tells you that you have said something offensive, this is an obvious moment to pause and consider the best way to handle the situation. Using your emotional intelligence, here are some steps to take.

Take a moment to pause

Being called out can put us on the defensive, so breathe deeply and remember that everyone makes mistakes. In most cases, committing a microaggression does not mean you are a bad person; it signals that you have a chance to treat a colleague with greater respect and to grow on your DEI journey.

Taking a moment to pause, breathe, and reflect can help you avoid reacting with emotion and potentially saying something rash that could make the situation worse.

Ask for clarification

If you are unsure what you did to offend your colleague, invite dialogue by asking for clarification. Say, "Could you say more about what you mean by that?"

Listen for understanding

Listen to your colleague's perspective, even when you disagree. Far too often in uncomfortable conversations, we listen for the opportunity to speak and insert our own opinions instead of truly listening for understanding. To make sure you have understood your colleague's point of view, you could restate or paraphrase what you heard: "I think I heard you saying _____ [paraphrase their comments]. Is that correct?"

Acknowledge and apologize

Once you process that harm has been done, you must acknowledge the offense and sincerely apologize for your statement. This is a moment to be honest, whether you lacked the knowledge of a certain word's history or made a comment that was insensitive. You could say something like, "I can now better understand how I was wrong in this situation. I will work to become more aware of _____ [the topic that you need to increase your cultural awareness of]."

Create space for follow-up

The majority of these tough conversations take more than one conversation to work through. Allow yourself and your colleagues the opportunity to follow up in the future to continue the conversation, especially when cooler heads can prevail. You may say something like, "I would be happy to talk about this more in the future if you have any follow-up thoughts. I appreciate you taking the time to share your perspective with me."

What Leaders Should Know

While microaggressions often happen at the individual level, companies that say they are committed to inclusion should have zero tolerance for exclusionary or discriminatory language toward any employee. Leaders should set the standard by providing training on topics such as microaggressions. Yet, because of the insidious nature of microaggressions, leaders and HR professionals have the responsibility to correct individuals when they become aware that these offenses have happened.

Many microaggressions can become part of an organization's culture if not corrected. For example, I have worked with some organizations where confusing people of the same race happened often and was casually overlooked as an honest mistake. While we all do make mistakes, when these same types of incidents happen consistently to the same groups of people, leaders need to correct the behavior. One client came to me with the issue that two Asian women on the same team were often called each other's name, giving them a feeling of interchangeability. I helped the client share with the firm some tools on how to politely correct someone in the moment, as well as provided some general reminders to the firm about why it's offensive to confuse two people of the same race. One thing that firm did was to push employees to learn each other's names and make sure to have individual interactions with new colleagues to get to know them. They even had a name challenge, with a prize, when they returned to the office after working remotely during the pandemic. In this way, the firm acted to not only call out inappropriate behavior but also shift the culture by making it clear that knowing colleagues' names was an important expectation for all team members.

Ultimately, getting better at noticing and responding to microaggressions—and at being more aware of our everyday speech—is a journey, one with a real effect on our mental health and well-being at work. Microaggressions affect everyone, so creating more inclusive and culturally competent workplace cultures means each of us must explore our own biases in order to become aware of them. The goal is not to be fearful of communicating with each other, but instead to embrace the opportunity to be intentional about it. Creating inclusive cultures where people can thrive does not happen overnight. It takes a continuous process of learning, evolving, and growing.

Adapted from hbr.org, May 10, 2022. Reprint H07195

Handling Fierce Criticism and Personal Attacks

An interview with Ruchika T. Malhotra and Patti Neuhold-Ravikumar by Amy Bernstein

I f you're in a leadership role, or any role where you're putting yourself and your ideas out there in an outspoken and visible way, chances are that at some point people are going to criticize you, sometimes fiercely, sometimes publicly. Are you ready for that?

Two women who've felt the heat because of decisions they've made or arguments they've put forward—or simply because of who they are—reflect on the ways they've steeled themselves for harsh or personal critiques and dealt with the fallout. *Women at Work* cohost Amy Bernstein spoke with Patti Neuhold-Ravikumar, an executive coach who was previously the president and CEO of the University of Central Oklahoma, and

Ruchika T. Malhotra, who is the founder of the inclusion strategy firm Candour. She is the author of *Inclusion on Purpose: An Intersectional Approach to Creating a Culture of Belonging at Work* and *Uncompete: Rejecting Competition to Unlock Success.* Neuhold-Ravikumar describes the preparation and the presence of mind she summoned as a university president communicating contentious budget cuts. Malhotra brings her expertise in DEI and women's leadership to contextualize those experiences, and she describes her own experiences with online harassment and how she's dealt with skeptics.

Both are experts on communicating strategically about difficult issues. Their stories of how they responded to fierce criticism will help you think about how you might respond—both when you see it coming and when you don't.

AMY BERNSTEIN: If you're in charge of an organization or in any role where you're visible and outspoken, chances are that people will criticize you, sometimes fiercely, sometimes publicly. Are you ready for that? Ruchika T. Malhotra wasn't, at least not at the beginning of her career as a finance journalist and advocate for diversity in business. She'd written an article about a new immigration category for the spouses of work visa holders, and in the comments section a reader called her the C word.

RUCHIKA T. MALHOTRA: I was absolutely shocked. None of my training as a journalist had prepared me for it. Much of what I *was* hearing was from male journalists who were like, "*Oh, just let it roll off your shoulders. It's no big deal.*" This nameless, faceless troll had just attacked me ad hominem for who I was. It was really painful. It's been well over a decade since that happened,

Idea in Brief

The Problem
Leaders and others in high-visibility positions often face fierce criticism and personal attacks both in person and online. This can be particularly acute for women and people of color, who may experience additional scrutiny and bias.

The Solution
To handle and respond to such harsh critiques, you need to prepare, listen with humility, and focus on the content rather than the emotional impact. Strategies include knowing your sources, pausing to collect yourself, practicing responses to tough questions, and maintaining a supportive community. Differentiate between personal attacks and feedback on decisions or outcomes.

The Benefits
By effectively managing criticism, you can demonstrate resilience, maintain your integrity, and foster a culture of honest debate and learning. This approach helps build your confidence and personal efficacy, improve decision-making, and create a supportive work environment.

---

and I wish I could say that was the last time, but as a woman on the internet, as a woman of color on the internet, it still happens regularly, often in more subtle ways now.

PATTI NEUHOLD-RAVIKUMAR: As a university president, you're also in the spotlight. Everything you say can and will be used in some way to either represent what you believe or feel or what you believe or feel in relationship to the university. So, you have to be thoughtful about your representation for the people who are leaning on you for leadership. The attention and scrutiny were intense, but I found ways to deal with it. When I think about criticism now, I ask myself, are they criticizing me as a person or are they criticizing a decision I've made? Are they criticizing an outcome that they're experiencing?

Our institution had a significant budget deficit, which is not unique in public higher education. But the situation had reached a fever pitch, and having been CFO prior to becoming president, I knew firsthand what had been done and what hadn't been done. We had run out of time pushing the problem off as long as we could. It was my responsibility in this new role to address it, and there were decisions I had to make to close this gap.

With the support of a great team and input from the rest of campus, we needed to stop spending more than we were bringing in. We had already eliminated dozens and dozens of staff positions. Due to the significant decrease in enrollment, we were at a place where we needed to let go some faculty positions.

Understandably so, that didn't sit well with the faculty—or our students. I learned one day that a student protest on this issue was going to march across campus to my office; the following afternoon my office was filled with more than 100 students who were not happy while a dozen faculty waited outside. They were armed with general but not fully accurate information. Trying to explain and assuage, while holding your footing—this is the tough stuff that we're all here to do.

I was in the news. Presidents from across the country were calling me because they had seen it. There were things that didn't feel good in those moments, but later when I stepped back and I rewatched the video and read the articles in the paper again, I listened to the student voices, and I thought, you know what, they're not criticizing me personally in most of this. It was really the *outcome* that they were criticizing. That helped me frame the moment for myself.

AMY: *That shows tremendous poise to be able to say,* This isn't about me. This is about a tough decision I had to make that's going to have a really tough impact on them.

RUCHIKA T. MALHOTRA: I'm wondering if you ever felt that being a woman impacted the level of criticism you got? Was there criticism around being a woman and the soundness of your decision-making?

PATTI: I never was dealing with someone who was so bold as to say, *"It's because you're a female."* I usually work so hard to assume that everything is coming from a neutral perspective that I overlook some barbs that are aimed at me in that way. I never felt it was directly aimed at me because I was a female, but I was criticized more heavily and probably challenged about my credentials more than the men. I remember in one of the protests, one of the students said, "Do you feel like you're competent to do your job?" And I thought, *I think I just heard somebody question whether I'm competent enough.* And I thought, *OK, well, I'm not going to be arrogant about this.* "Of course," I answered the question. "Yes, of course I believe I'm competent to do this." But have they asked that of any previous president? I don't think so.

So, Ruchika, I wish I could say it was completely neutral, but I think there are a lot of influences there. I'm also a gay female, and that adds another layer, subconsciously for some people, politically for other people.

AMY: So, you were starting to piece together what might've been a pattern. Did that soften the blow for you or how did it affect the way you felt in the moment?

PATTI: Well, I felt like there was a team of other people in the world that needed me to be courageous in that moment. I knew that my campus and the young students needed to see what honest debate and different points of view looked like. But I felt like in that moment, I needed to stay steadfast. I had to be "the woman in the arena," to paraphrase Theodore Roosevelt. I literally was surrounded by these students, and this was their opportunity to see how to handle being questioned and being criticized, and how to handle a moment when you disagree with so many people and you're feeling that heat.

RUCHIKA: A lot of the traditional management and leadership advice—*"Criticism is good," "You can't be liked* and *respected," "It's fine, just get over it"*—has never resonated with me. I see it with women leaders, leaders of color, leaders with other historically excluded identities. This kind of advice is reserved for people who have not historically had their authority questioned.

I have also received criticism on my competence when I've taught at universities. In a class of 20, I can receive 18 student evaluations that say, *"This is wonderful. This was a great course. I learned a lot."* And there'll be two that say, *"Is she even qualified to teach?"* or *"I didn't like this class."* The last decade for me has been focused on figuring out how to unlearn the notion that I have to be likable and palatable to everyone.

At some point you just have to realize that there are going to be people who are just not going to like the message. Some of us have to understand that even though the message might be sound, there will always be people who are going to be challenged and triggered by the fact that someone in this package is delivering this message. And you have to be OK with that.

PATTI: It stings when people attack you personally. But you have to have the courage to be disliked. And that's something that I think we're not so practiced at doing.

AMY: Let's talk about how we go about taking this moment of attack, of criticism, and processing it so that we can deal with it in a way that is constructive. Patti, when people came after you, often with wrong information, how did you process that?

PATTI: No matter how much you think you're ready for it, or how much you've practiced or prepared, it's never easy. But you typically know when those moments are coming: You've said something that challenges other people's beliefs, or you have an issue on the table that's causing disagreement in some way.

Start with preparation, knowing your sources, and expecting tough questions. To me, preparation means knowing where I'm getting my data when I'm saying things that I believe are factual. And not only do I need the data, I need to have sources ready. I was in a community of people who wanted to know why, where, and how about most everything. I had somebody help me practice by asking me tough questions that might come my way. So I had prepared my mind not to be shocked or caught off guard.

In the moment, listen honestly and with humility. It's really hard to listen honestly when you've already made or shared a decision, statement, or commitment. Strive to hear other people and to understand that there may be other perspectives or hidden impact on a broader group. It's important to have them be aware that you are listening to feedback and criticism.

Next, focus on what was said rather than how it makes you feel. My dad taught me that there were times when he would say something and I'd hear it much more critically than what he intended. But if I just listened to the words, I could turn down my feeling meter a little bit and say, "OK, it's not as sensitive as I'm making it. I just need to get over that first emotional hump."

And finally, is to rise above your circumstances. These things are what they are. I may not be able to change anything about what is happening in this moment, but I have the power to react in a way that is representative of me, my beliefs, and my values, and puts my best foot forward.

AMY: The part about hearing what was actually said makes a lot of sense to me when people are asking "Why are you making those cuts?" Does it play in at all when someone is questioning your competence?

PATTI: It's more challenging in those moments. In that particular moment with the student, I had to remember that we are in an environment that is designed for people to be challenged with new ideas and with ideals that we don't agree with. If you can't have a protest on a college campus, where the heck can you? I didn't want to squelch the opportunity these students had to learn how to express their displeasure, how to share and receive information, and how to challenge somebody. It's OK to challenge someone in authority.

My part was to make sure I participated in this event, and that meant answering their questions. I didn't feel that it would be helpful to avoid questions, whether they were about me or about what was going on in the moment. I knew that my answer to the question about my competence would set the stage for questions that came later. So it was important for me to say, "Yes, I'm competent," and then to look to the next person who had a question. If I had given that student a cross look or made a face, that would've been the news story.

I think this time of instant video, social media, and the immediate news scoop has removed an essential part of our response and conversational negotiating—a pause. When somebody hears information and immediately shares it on the internet, they haven't stopped to think about it, process it, or ask questions. So when we're put on the spot in those moments, we have to quickly *create* that pause to let our minds catch up and our emotions tune down. In that moment in my office with the students, I had to turn down the emotions, breathe, and respond.

AMY: One way I have found to do that is to say, "That's a really interesting question. Give me a second to think about that." Even though what's going through my mind is, *Oh, my God, get me out of here!*

RUCHIKA: I find so much in common with Patti in my own experiences of criticism. Now, when someone makes an ad hominem attack on me, as a woman or a person of color, I've had to categorize that as bullying. They had their own feelings about who I was, and it has very little to do with me.

I've also been criticized for the work I've done in talking about equity and inclusion. Patti, I loved what you said about being prepared. Having a community around you to check in with and bolster you in these moments is super important. When I wrote my first book on gender bias in the workplace, it was helpful to have people in my community ask me questions I knew I would face such as *"Don't you think that if the gender pay gap was real, every organization would just hire women because it would be so much cheaper to do that?"* I knew when I got on stage I was going to face that question or criticism of my arguments. With the support of my community, it was easier to separate out what was a criticism of my argument rather than me personally.

Amy, I'm really curious, are there situations where you've faced the fire, and how have you dealt with it?

AMY: I haven't been in the situation either of you has been in, never anything close. There was a time when I was a new manager and a junior member of a very large team I oversaw walked into my office, sat down in front of my desk, and said something like, "A bunch of us wanted to give you a piece of feedback." I have to admit, the moment I heard feedback, I thought, *Oh God, it's the F word. I don't want feedback*. But what I said was, "OK, what's the feedback?" It was that people didn't like that I always seemed to be multitasking and never paying attention to them when they needed me to. As it happened, as I was receiving this piece of feedback, I was answering email.

So, as I'm hearing this criticism, my first response was definitely fight or flight. I could feel my heart racing. I could feel my anger rising, and I just wanted to walk out of my own office and shut the door behind me. But I was able to take a breath and say, "You know what, you're absolutely right. You're not the first person who's pointed this out to me. Shame on me for not correcting this behavior."

It took guts for this junior member of my team to walk into her new boss's office to deliver this message. I hated thinking that that's what my management boiled down to for so many people. In the end, I had to just own that. So thereafter, whenever anyone walks into my office, I shut my laptop, partly to say I'm listening to you, partly to keep my eye from wandering to the screen. I had to tame myself that way.

PATTI: I appreciate that I didn't hear an apology in what you said to that person. You responded and accepted the criticism and the possibility that it was legitimate and real. If it's constructive criticism, they're not looking for an apology; they're looking for change, and you gave it to them.

RUCHIKA: Another important part of what I heard is that if you're hearing feedback and criticism from multiple sources, then pay attention. It's different if one person says something out of the blue that catches you caught off guard, versus hearing echoes of this criticism or feedback from various people.

AMY: What does it look like when criticism leads to pressure to walk back a decision?

RUCHIKA: Amy Edmondson's work around both psychological safety and intelligent failures is very relevant. So you make a decision, you come under fire, and then you say, "OK, I've actually thought about it." And if you *do* need to walk back or change a decision, you could be seen as a person who's indecisive. A lot of the criticism around that is gender bias as well. Therese Huston's research shows that women actually make great decisions, and we do take calculated risks really well.

PATTI: Anecdotally, I think that women deal with this by spending more time than their male counterparts trying to build support for an idea before they launch that decision.

RUCHIKA: I'm so glad you said that because that is another area where I think the existing leadership advice is bad: "Be unflappable," "Never question a decision," "You don't need to build consensus because leaders make hard decisions." That's not only bad advice—it's especially harmful for leaders who are the first or the few or the only.

AMY: Sometimes you do need to walk back a decision. You learned something you didn't know that you should have known, and you have to take responsibility for that. But walking back a decision isn't weak leadership in and of itself.

PATTI: No. It shows that you listen, that you can be persuaded, that you can adapt as facts and reality change, that you have to be an agile decision-maker to know that at any moment the factors can change and that decision may no longer be sound.

> **Adapted from "The Essentials: Handling Fierce Criticism,"**
> ***Women at Work podcast*, March 25, 2024.**

The Making of a Corporate Athlete

by Jim Loehr and Tony Schwartz

If there is one quality that executives seek for themselves and their employees, it is sustained high performance in the face of ever-increasing pressure and rapid change. But the source of such performance is as elusive as the fountain of youth. Management theorists have long sought to identify precisely what makes some people flourish under pressure and others fold. We maintain that they have come up with only partial answers: rich material rewards, the right culture, management by objectives.

The problem with most approaches, we believe, is that they deal with people only from the neck up, connecting high performance primarily with cognitive capacity. In recent years there has been a growing focus on the relationship between emotional intelligence and high performance. A few theorists have addressed the spiritual dimension—how deeper values and a sense of purpose influence performance. Almost no one has paid any attention to the role played by physical capacities. A successful approach to sustained high performance, we have found, must pull together all of these elements and consider the person as a whole. Thus, our integrated theory of performance management addresses the body, the emotions, the mind, and the spirit. We call this hierarchy the *performance pyramid*. Each of its levels profoundly influences the others, and failure to address any one of them compromises performance.

Our approach has its roots in the two decades that Jim Loehr and his colleagues at LGE spent working with world-class athletes. Several years ago, the two of us began to develop a more comprehensive version of these techniques for executives facing unprecedented demands in the workplace. In effect, we realized, these executives are "corporate athletes." If they were to perform at high levels over the long haul, we posited, they would have to train in the same systematic, multilevel way that world-class athletes do. We have now tested our model on thousands of executives. Their dramatically improved work performance and their enhanced health and happiness confirm our initial hypothesis. In the pages that follow, we describe our approach in detail.

Ideal Performance State

In training athletes, we have never focused on their primary skills—how to hit a serve, swing a golf club, or shoot a basketball. Likewise, in business we don't address primary competencies such as public speaking, negotiating, or analyzing a balance sheet. Our efforts aim instead to help executives build their capacity for what might be called supportive or secondary competencies, among them endurance, strength, flexibility, self-control, and focus. Increasing capacity at all levels allows

Idea in Brief

The Problem

Sustained high achievement demands physical and emotional strength as well as a sharp intellect. Executives need to learn what world-class athletes already know: Recovering energy is as important as expending it.

The Solution

To perform at high levels over multiple decades, executives must train in the systematic, multilevel way that athletes do. Physical capacity is the foundation, with emotional, mental, and spiritual capacity layered on it. Leaders must manage their energy through oscillation—rhythmic movement between stress and recovery. Rituals that promote physical fitness, emotional resilience, mental focus, and spiritual purpose are essential for achieving the Ideal Performance State.

The Benefits

Executives who use the model increase professional performance and improve the quality of their lives. In an ever-changing environment, performing consistently at high levels is now more necessary.

---

athletes and executives alike to bring their talents and skills to full ignition and to sustain high performance over time—a condition we call the *Ideal Performance State* (IPS). Obviously, executives can perform successfully even if they smoke, drink and weigh too much, or lack emotional skills or a higher purpose for working. But they cannot perform to their full potential or without a cost over time—to themselves, to their families, and to the corporations for which they work. Put simply, the best long-term performers tap into positive energy at all levels of the performance pyramid.

Extensive research in sports science has confirmed that the capacity to mobilize energy on demand is the foundation of IPS. Our own work has demonstrated that effective energy

The high-performance pyramid

Peak performance in business has often been presented as a matter of sheer brainpower, but we view performance as a pyramid. Physical well-being is its foundation. Above that rests emotional health, then mental acuity, and at the top, a sense of purpose. The Ideal Performance State—peak performance under pressure—is achieved when all levels are working together.

Rituals that promote oscillation—the rhythmic expenditure and recovery of energy—link the levels of the pyramid. For instance, vigorous exercise can produce a sense of emotional well-being, clearing the way for peak mental performance.

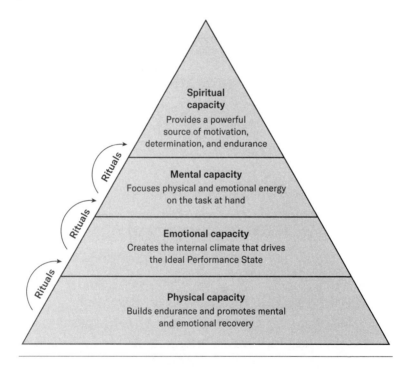

management has two key components. The first is the rhythmic movement between energy expenditure (stress) and energy renewal (recovery), which we term "oscillation." In the living laboratory of sports, we learned that the real enemy of high performance is not stress, which, paradoxical as it may seem, is actually the stimulus for growth. Rather, the problem is the absence of disciplined, intermittent recovery. Chronic stress without recovery depletes energy reserves, leads to burnout and breakdown, and ultimately undermines performance. Rituals that promote oscillation—rhythmic stress and recovery—are the second component of high performance. Repeated regularly, these highly precise, consciously developed routines become automatic over time.

The same methods that enable world-class athletes to reach IPS under pressure, we theorized, would be at least equally effective for business leaders—and perhaps even more important in their lives. The demands on executives to sustain high performance day in and day out, year in and year out, dwarf the challenges faced by any athlete we have ever trained. The average professional athlete, for example, spends most of his time practicing and only a small percentage—several hours a day, at most—actually competing. The typical executive, by contrast, devotes almost no time to training and must perform on demand ten, 12, 14 hours a day or more. Athletes enjoy several months of off-season, while most executives are fortunate to get three or four weeks of vacation a year. The career of the average professional athlete spans seven years; the average executive can expect to work 40 to 50 years.

Of course, even corporate athletes who train at all levels will have bad days and run into challenges they can't overcome. Life is tough, and for many time-starved executives, it is only getting tougher. But that is precisely our point. While it isn't always in our power to change our external conditions, we can train to better manage our inner state. We aim to help corporate athletes use the full range of their capacities to thrive in the most difficult circumstances and to emerge from stressful periods stronger, healthier, and eager for the next challenge.

Physical Capacity

Energy can be defined most simply as the capacity to do work. Our training process begins at the physical level because the body is our fundamental source of energy—the foundation of the performance pyramid. Perhaps the best paradigm for building capacity is weight lifting. Several decades of sports science research have established that the key to increasing physical strength is a phenomenon known as supercompensation—essentially the creation of balanced work-rest ratios. In weight lifting, this involves stressing a muscle to the point where its fibers literally start to break down. Given an adequate period of recovery (typically at least 48 hours), the muscle will not only heal, it will grow stronger. But persist in stressing the muscle without rest and the result will be acute and chronic damage. Conversely, failure to stress the muscle results in weakness and atrophy. (Just think of an arm in a cast for several weeks.) In both cases, the enemy is not stress, it's linearity—the failure to oscillate between energy expenditure and recovery.

We first understood the power of rituals to prompt recovery by observing world-class tennis players in the crucible of match play. The best competitors, we discovered, use precise recovery rituals in the 15 or 20 seconds *between* points—often without even being aware of it. Their between-point routines include concentrating on the strings of their rackets to avoid distraction, assuming a confident posture, and visualizing how they want the next point to play out. These routines have startling physiological effects. When we hooked players up to heart rate monitors during their matches, the competitors with the most consistent rituals showed dramatic oscillation, their heart rates rising rapidly during play and then dropping as much as 15% to 20% between points.

The mental and emotional effects of precise between-point routines are equally significant. They allow players to avoid negative feelings, focus their minds, and prepare for the next point. By contrast, players who lack between-point rituals, or who practice them inconsistently, become linear—they expend too much energy without recovery. Regardless of their talent or level of fitness, they become more vulnerable to frustration, anxiety, and loss of concentration and far more likely to choke under pressure.

The same lesson applies to the corporate athletes we train. The problem, we explain, is not so much that their lives are increasingly stressful as that they are so relentlessly linear. Typically, they push themselves too hard mentally and emotionally and too little physically. Both forms of linearity undermine performance.

When we began working with Marilyn Clark, a managing director of Salomon Smith Barney, she had almost no oscillation in her life. Clark, who is in her late 30s, runs the firm's Cleveland office. She is also the mother of three young children, and her husband is a high-powered executive in his own right. To all appearances, Clark lives an enviable life, and she was loath to complain about it. Yet her hectic lifestyle was exacting a cost, which became clear after some probing. In the mornings, temporarily fueled by coffee and a muffin, she was alert and energetic. By the afternoon, though, her energy sagged, and she got through the rest of the day on sheer willpower. At lunchtime, when she could have taken a few quiet moments to recover, she found that she couldn't say no to employees who lined up at her office seeking counsel and support. Between the demands of her job, her colleagues, and her family, she had almost no time for herself. Her frustration quietly grew.

We began our work with Clark by taking stock of her physical capacity. While she had been a passionate athlete as a teenager and an All-American lacrosse player in college, her fitness regimen for the past several years had been limited to occasional sit-ups before bedtime. As she learned more about the relationship between energy and high performance, Clark agreed that her first priority was to get back in shape. She wanted to feel better physically, and she knew from past experience that her mood would improve if she built regular workouts into her schedule.

Because old habits die hard, we helped Clark establish positive rituals to replace them. Part of the work was creating a supportive environment. The colleagues with whom Clark trained became a source of cheerleading—and even nagging—as she established a routine that would have previously seemed unthinkable. Clark committed to work out in a nearby gym three days a week, precisely at 1 p.m. She also enlisted her husband to watch the kids so that she could get in a workout on Saturdays and Sundays.

Regular workouts have helped Clark create clear work-life boundaries and restored her sense of herself as an athlete. Now, rather than tumbling into an energy trough in the afternoons and reaching for a candy bar, Clark returns to the office from her workouts feeling reenergized and better able to focus. Physical stress has become a source not just of greater endurance but also of emotional and mental recovery; Clark finds that she can work fewer hours and get more done. And finally, because she no longer feels chronically overburdened, she believes that she has become a better boss. "My body feels reawakened," she says. "I'm much more relaxed, and the resentment I was feeling about all the demands on me is gone."

Clark has inspired other members of her firm to take out health club memberships. She and several colleagues are subsidizing employees who can't easily afford the cost. "We're not just talking to each other about business accolades and who is covering which account," she says. "Now it's also about whether we got our workouts in and how well we're recovering. We're sharing something healthy, and that has brought people together."

The corporate athlete doesn't build a strong physical foundation by exercise alone, of course. Good sleeping and eating rituals are integral to effective energy management. When we first met Rudy Borneo, the vice chairman of Macy's West, he complained of erratic energy levels, wide mood swings, and difficulty concentrating. He was also overweight. Like many executives—and most Americans—his eating habits were poor. He typically began his long, travel-crammed days by skipping breakfast—the equivalent of rolling to the start line of the Indianapolis 500 with a near-empty fuel tank. Lunch was catch-as-catch-can, and Borneo used sugary snacks to fight off his inevitable afternoon hunger pangs. These foods spiked his blood glucose levels, giving him a quick jolt of energy, but one that faded quickly. Dinner was often a rich, multicourse meal eaten late in the evening. Digesting that much food disturbed Borneo's sleep and left him feeling sluggish and out of sorts in the mornings.

Sound familiar?

As we did with Clark, we helped Borneo replace his bad habits with positive rituals, beginning with the way he ate. We explained that by eating lightly but often, he could sustain a steady level of energy. (For a fuller account of the foundational exercise, eating, and sleep routines, see the sidebar "A Firm Foundation.") Borneo now eats breakfast every day—typically a high-protein drink rather than coffee and a bagel. We also showed him research by chronobiologists suggesting that the body and mind need recovery every 90 to 120 minutes. Using that cycle as the

A Firm Foundation

Here are our basic strategies for renewing energy at the physical level. Some of them are so familiar they've become background noise, easy to ignore. That's why we're repeating them. If any of these strategies aren't part of your life now, their absence may help account for fatigue, irritability, lack of emotional resilience, difficulty concentrating, and even a flagging sense of purpose.

1. Actually do all those healthy things you know you ought to do

Eat five or six small meals a day; people who eat just one or two meals a day with long periods in between force their bodies into a conservation mode, which translates into slower metabolism. Always eat breakfast: eating first thing in the morning sends your body the signal that it need not slow metabolism to conserve energy. Eat a balanced diet. Despite all the conflicting nutritional research, overwhelming evidence suggests that a healthy dietary ratio is 50% to 60% complex carbohydrates, 25% to 35% protein, and 20% to 25% fat. Dramatically reduce simple sugars. In addition to representing empty calories, sugar causes energy-depleting spikes in blood glucose levels. Drink four to five 12-ounce glasses of water daily, even if you don't feel thirsty. As much as half the population walks around with mild chronic dehydration. And finally, on the "you know you should" list: get physically active. We strongly recommend three to four 20- to 30-minute cardiovascular workouts a week, including at least two sessions of intervals—short bursts of intense exertion followed by brief recovery periods.

---

basis for his eating schedule, he installed a refrigerator by his desk and began eating five or six small but nutritious meals a day and sipping water frequently. He also shifted the emphasis in his workouts to interval training, which increased his endurance and speed of recovery.

2. Go to bed early and wake up early

Night owls have a much more difficult time dealing with the demands of today's business world, because typically, they still have to get up with the early birds. They're often groggy and unfocused in the mornings, dependent on caffeine and sugary snacks to keep up their energy. You can establish new sleep rituals. Biological clocks are not fixed in our genes.

3. Maintain a consistent bedtime and wake-up time

As important as the number of hours you sleep (ideally seven to eight) is the consistency of the recovery wave you create. Regular sleep cycles help regulate your other biological clocks and increase the likelihood that the sleep you get will be deep and restful.

4. Seek recovery every 90 to 120 minutes

Chronobiologists have found that the body's hormone, glucose, and blood pressure levels drop every 90 minutes or so. By failing to seek recovery and overriding the body's natural stress-rest cycles, overall capacity is compromised. As we've learned from athletes, even short, focused breaks can promote significant recovery. We suggest five sources of restoration: eat something, hydrate, move physically, change channels mentally, and change channels emotionally.

5. Do at least two weight-training workouts a week

No form of exercise more powerfully turns back the markers of age than weight training. It increases strength, retards osteoporosis, speeds up metabolism, enhances mobility, improves posture, and dramatically increases energy.

In addition to prompting weight loss and making him feel better, Borneo's nutritional and fitness rituals have had a dramatic effect on other aspects of his life. "I now exercise for my mind as much as for my body," he says. "At the age of 59, I have more energy than ever, and I can sustain it for a longer period of time.

For me, the rituals are the holy grail. Using them to create balance has had an impact on every aspect of my life: staying more positive, handling difficult human resource issues, dealing with change, treating people better. I really do believe that when you learn to take care of yourself, you free up energy and enthusiasm to care more for others."

Emotional Capacity

The next building block of IPS is emotional capacity—the internal climate that supports peak performance. During our early research, we asked hundreds of athletes to describe how they felt when they were performing at their best. Invariably, they used words such as "calm," "challenged," "engaged," "focused," "optimistic," and "confident." As sprinter Marion Jones put it shortly after winning one of her gold medals at the Olympic Games in Sydney: "I'm out here having a ball. This is not a stressful time in my life. This is a very happy time." When we later asked the same question of law enforcement officers, military personnel, surgeons, and corporate executives, they used remarkably similar language to describe their Ideal Performance State.

Just as positive emotions ignite the energy that drives high performance, negative emotions—frustration, impatience, anger, fear, resentment, and sadness—drain energy. Over time, these feelings can be literally toxic, elevating heart rate and blood pressure, increasing muscle tension, constricting vision, and ultimately crippling performance. Anxious, fear ridden athletes are far more likely to choke in competition, for example, while anger and frustration sabotage their capacity for calm focus.

The impact of negative emotions on business performance is subtler but no less devastating. Alan, an executive at an investment company, travels frequently, overseeing a half-dozen offices around the country. His colleagues and subordinates, we learned, considered him to be a perfectionist and an often critical boss whose frustration and impatience sometimes boiled over into angry tirades. Our work focused on helping Alan find ways to manage his emotions more effectively. His anger, we explained, was a reactive emotion, a fight-or-flight response to situations he perceived as threatening. To manage more effectively, he needed to transform his inner experience of threat under stress into one of challenge.

A regular workout regimen built Alan's endurance and gave him a way to burn off tension. But because his fierce travel schedule often got in the way of his workouts, we also helped him develop a precise five-step ritual to contain his negative emotions whenever they threatened to erupt. His initial challenge was to become more aware of signals from his body that he was on edge—physical tension, a racing heart, tightness in his chest. When he felt those sensations arise, his first step was to close his eyes and take several deep breaths. Next, he consciously relaxed the muscles in his face. Then, he made an effort to soften his voice and speak more slowly. After that, he tried to put himself in the shoes of the person who was the target of his anger—to imagine what he or she must be feeling. Finally, he focused on framing his response in positive language.

Instituting this ritual felt awkward to Alan at first, not unlike trying to learn a new golf swing. More than once he reverted to his old behavior. But within several weeks, the five-step drill had become automatic—a highly reliable way to short-circuit his reactivity. Numerous employees reported that he had become more reasonable, more approachable, and less scary. Alan himself says that he has become a far more effective manager.

Through our work with athletes, we have learned a number of other rituals that help to offset feelings of stress and restore positive energy. It's no coincidence, for example, that many athletes wear headphones as they prepare for competition. Music has powerful physiological and emotional effects. It can prompt a shift in mental activity from the rational left hemisphere of the brain to the more intuitive right hemisphere. It also provides a relief from obsessive thinking and worrying. Finally, music can be a means of directly regulating energy—raising it when the time comes to perform and lowering it when it is more appropriate to decompress.

Body language also influences emotions. In one well-known experiment, actors were asked to portray anger and then were subjected to numerous physiological tests, including heart rate, blood pressure, core temperature, galvanic skin response, and hormone levels. Next, the actors were exposed to a situation that made them genuinely angry, and the same measurements were taken. There were virtually no differences in the two profiles. Effective acting produces precisely the same physiology that real emotions do. All great athletes understand this instinctively. If they carry themselves confidently, they will eventually start to feel confident, even in highly stressful situations. That's why we train our corporate clients to "act as if"—consciously creating the look on the outside that they want to feel on the inside. "You are what you repeatedly do," said Aristotle. "Excellence is not a singular act but a habit."

Close relationships are perhaps the most powerful means for prompting positive emotions and effective recovery. Anyone who has enjoyed a happy family reunion or an evening with good friends knows the profound sense of safety and security that these relationships can induce. Such feelings are closely associated with the Ideal Performance State. Unfortunately, many of the corporate athletes we train believe that in order to perform up to expectations at work, they have no choice but to stint on their time with loved ones. We try to reframe the issue. By devoting more time to their most important relationships and setting clearer boundaries between work and home, we tell our clients, they will not only derive more satisfaction but will also get the recovery that they need to perform better at work.

Mental Capacity

The third level of the performance pyramid—the cognitive—is where most traditional performance-enhancement training is aimed. The usual approaches tend to focus on improving competencies by using techniques such as process reengineering and knowledge management or by learning to use more sophisticated technology. Our training aims to enhance our clients' cognitive capacities—most notably their focus, time management, and positive-and critical-thinking skills.

Focus simply means energy concentrated in the service of a particular goal. Anything that interferes with focus dissipates energy. Meditation, typically viewed as a spiritual practice, can serve as a highly practical means of training attention and promoting recovery. At this level, no guidance from a guru is required. A perfectly adequate meditation technique involves sitting quietly and breathing deeply, counting each exhalation, and starting over when you reach ten. Alternatively, you can choose a word to repeat each time you take a breath.

Practiced regularly, meditation quiets the mind, the emotions, and the body, promoting energy recovery. Numerous studies have shown, for example, that experienced meditators need considerably fewer hours of sleep than nonmeditators. Meditation and other noncognitive disciplines can also slow brain wave activity and stimulate a shift in mental activity from the left hemisphere of the brain to the right. Have you ever suddenly found the solution to a vexing problem while doing something "mindless" such as jogging, working in the garden, or singing in the shower? That's the left-brain, right-brain shift at work—the fruit of mental oscillation.

Much of our training at this level focuses on helping corporate athletes to consciously manage their time and energy. By alternating periods of stress with renewal, they learn to align their work with the body's need for breaks every 90 to 120 minutes. This can be challenging for compulsive corporate achievers. Jeffrey Sklar, 39, managing director for institutional sales at the New York investment firm Gruntal & Company, had long been accustomed to topping his competitors by brute force—pushing harder and more relentlessly than anyone else. With our help, he built a set of rituals that ensured regular recovery and also enabled him to perform at a higher level while spending fewer hours at work.

Once in the morning and again in the afternoon, Sklar retreats from the frenetic trading floor to a quiet office, where he spends 15 minutes doing deep-breathing exercises. At lunch, he leaves the office—something he once would have found unthinkable—and walks outdoors for at least 15 minutes. He also works out five or six times a week after work. At home, he and his wife, Sherry, a busy executive herself, made a pact never to talk business after 8 p.m. They also swore off work on the weekends, and they have stuck to their vow for nearly two years. During each of those years, Sklar's earnings have increased by more than 65%.

For Jim Connor, the president and CEO of FootJoy, reprioritizing his time became a way not just to manage his energy better but to create more balance in his life and to revive his sense of passion. Connor had come to us saying that he felt stuck in a deep rut. "My feelings were muted so I could deal with the emotional pain of life," he explains. "I had smoothed out all the vicissitudes in my life to such an extent that oscillation was prohibited. I was not feeling life but repetitively performing it."

Connor had imposed on himself the stricture that he be the first person to arrive at the office each day and the last to leave. In reality, he acknowledged, no one would object if he arrived a little later or left a little earlier a couple of days a week. He realized it also made sense for him to spend one or two days a week working at a satellite plant 45 minutes nearer to his home than his main office. Doing so could boost morale at the second plant while cutting 90 minutes from his commute.

Immediately after working with us, Connor arranged to have an office cleared out at the satellite factory. He now spends at least one full day a week there, prompting a number of people at that office to comment to him about his increased availability. He began taking a golf lesson one morning a week, which also allowed for a more relaxed drive to his main office, since he commutes there after rush hour on golf days. In addition, he instituted a monthly getaway routine with his wife. In the evenings, he often leaves his office earlier in order to spend more time with his family.

Connor has also meticulously built recovery into his workdays. "What a difference these fruit and water breaks make," he says. "I set my alarm watch for 90 minutes to prevent relapses, but I'm instinctively incorporating this routine into my life and love it. I'm far more productive as a result, and the quality of my thought process is measurably improved. I'm also doing more on the big things at work and not getting bogged down in detail. I'm pausing more to think and to take time out."

Rituals that encourage positive thinking also increase the likelihood of accessing the Ideal Performance State. Once again, our work with top athletes has taught us the power of creating specific mental rituals to sustain positive energy. Jack Nicklaus, one of the greatest pressure performers in the history of golf, seems to have an intuitive understanding of the importance of both oscillation and rituals. "I've developed a regimen that allows me to move from peaks of concentration into valleys of relaxation and back again as necessary," he wrote in *Golf Digest*. "My focus begins to sharpen as I walk onto the tee and steadily intensifies . . . until I hit [my drive] . . . I descend into a valley as I leave the tee, either through casual conversation with a fellow competitor or by letting my mind dwell on whatever happens into it."

Visualization is another ritual that produces positive energy and has palpable performance results. For example, Earl Woods taught his son Tiger—Nicklaus's heir apparent—to form a mental image of the ball rolling into the hole before each shot. The exercise does more than produce a vague feeling of optimism and well-being. Neuroscientist Ian Robertson of Trinity College, Dublin, author of *Mind Sculpture,* has found that visualization can literally reprogram the neural circuitry of the brain, directly improving performance. It is hard to imagine a better illustration than diver Laura Wilkinson. Six months before the summer Olympics in Sydney, Wilkinson broke three toes on her right foot while training. Unable to go in the water because of her cast, she instead spent hours a day on the diving platform, visualizing each of her dives. With only a few weeks to actually practice before the Olympics, she pulled off a huge upset, winning the gold medal on the ten-meter platform.

Visualization works just as well in the office. Sherry Sklar has a ritual to prepare for any significant event in her work life. "I always take time to sit down in advance in a quiet place and think about what I really want from the meeting," she says. "Then I visualize myself achieving the outcome I'm after." In effect, Sklar is building mental muscles—increasing her strength, endurance, and flexibility. By doing so, she decreases the likelihood that she will be distracted by negative thoughts under pressure. "It has made me much more relaxed and confident when I go into presentations," she says.

Spiritual Capacity

Most executives are wary of addressing the spiritual level of the performance pyramid in business settings, and understandably so. The word "spiritual" prompts conflicting emotions and doesn't seem immediately relevant to high performance. So let's be clear: by spiritual capacity, we simply mean the energy that is unleashed by tapping into one's deepest values and defining a strong sense of purpose. This capacity, we have found, serves as sustenance in the face of adversity and as a powerful source of motivation, focus, determination, and resilience.

Consider the case of Ann, a high-level executive at a large cosmetics company. For much of her adult life, she has tried unsuccessfully to quit smoking, blaming her failures on a lack of self-discipline. Smoking took a visible toll on her health and her productivity at work—decreased endurance from shortness of breath, more sick days than her colleagues, and nicotine cravings that distracted her during long meetings.

Four years ago, when Ann became pregnant, she was able to quit immediately and didn't touch a cigarette until the day her child was born, when she began smoking again. A year later, Ann became pregnant for a second time, and again she stopped smoking, with virtually no symptoms of withdrawal. True to her pattern, she resumed smoking when her child was born. "I don't understand it," she told us plaintively.

We offered a simple explanation. As long as Ann was able to connect the impact of smoking to a deeper purpose—the health of her unborn child—quitting was easy. She was able to make what we call a "values-based adaptation." But without a strong connection to a deeper sense of purpose, she went back to smoking—an expedient adaptation that served her short-term interests. Smoking was a sensory pleasure for Ann, as well as a way to allay her anxiety and manage social stress. Understanding cognitively that it was unhealthy, feeling guilty about it on an emotional level, and even experiencing its negative effects physically were all insufficient motivations to change her behavior. To succeed, Ann needed a more sustaining source of motivation.

Making such a connection, we have found, requires regularly stepping off the endless treadmill of deadlines and obligations to take time for reflection. The inclination for busy executives is to live in a perpetual state of triage, doing whatever seems most immediately pressing while losing sight of any bigger picture. Rituals that give people the opportunity to pause and look inside include meditation, journal writing, prayer, and service to others. Each of these activities can also serve as a source of recovery—a way to break the linearity of relentless goal-oriented activity.

Taking the time to connect to one's deepest values can be extremely rewarding. It can also be painful, as a client we'll call Richard discovered. Richard is a stockbroker who works in New York City and lives in a distant suburb, where his wife stays at home with their three young children. Between his long commute and his long hours, Richard spent little time with his family. Like so many of our clients, he typically left home before his children woke up and returned around 7:30 in the evening, feeling exhausted and in no mood to talk to anyone. He wasn't happy with his situation, but he saw no easy solution. In time, his unhappiness began to affect his work, which made him even more negative when he got home at night. It was a vicious cycle.

One evening while driving home from work, Richard found himself brooding about his life. Suddenly, he felt so overcome by emotion that he stopped his car at a park ten blocks from home to collect himself. To his astonishment, he began to weep. He felt consumed with grief about his life and filled with longing for his family. After ten minutes, all Richard wanted to do was get home and hug his wife and children. Accustomed to giving their dad a wide berth at the end of the day, his kids were understandably bewildered when he walked in that evening with tears streaming down his face and wrapped them all in hugs. When his wife arrived on the scene, her first thought was that he'd been fired.

The next day, Richard again felt oddly compelled to stop at the park near his house. Sure enough, the tears returned and so did the longing. Once again, he rushed home to his family. During the subsequent two years, Richard was able to count on one hand the number of times that he failed to stop at the same location for at least ten minutes. The rush of emotion subsided over time, but his sense that he was affirming what mattered most in his life remained as strong as ever.

Richard had stumbled into a ritual that allowed him both to disengage from work and to tap into a profound source of purpose and meaning—his family. In that context, going home ceased to be a burden after a long day and became instead a source of recovery and renewal. In turn, Richard's distraction at work diminished, and he became more focused, positive, and productive—so much so that he was able to cut down on his hours. On a practical level, he created a better balance between stress and recovery. Finally, by tapping into a deeper sense of purpose, he found a powerful new source of energy for both his work and his family.

In a corporate environment that is changing at warp speed, performing consistently at high levels is more difficult and more necessary than ever. Narrow interventions simply aren't sufficient anymore. Companies can't afford to address their employees' cognitive capacities while ignoring their physical, emotional, and spiritual well-being. On the playing field or in the boardroom, high performance depends as much on how people renew and recover energy as on how they expend it, on how they manage their lives as much as on how they manage their work. When people feel strong and resilient—physically, mentally, emotionally, and spiritually—they perform better, with more passion, for longer. They win, their families win, and the corporations that employ them win.

Originally published in January 2001. Reprint R0101H

9

Why Career Transition Is So Hard

by Herminia Ibarra

Today people at all stages of their careers are asking themselves profound questions about the kind of work they do, how much of it they want to do, and the place it occupies in their lives. We're asking ourselves these questions in part because fewer and fewer of us conceive of life as having the three "traditional" stages: a short early stage devoted to learning, a long middle stage dedicated to work, and a later stage devoted to enjoying one's golden years. Instead, with growing frequency, we're alternating between changing jobs and careers, pursuing opportunities for education, and making time for periods of rest and restoration.

This isn't a midlife-crisis type of questioning that flares up at a certain age and gets resolved once and for all. The accelerated pace of technological change and, most recently, the advent of AI are reshaping jobs and organizations in ways that call for constant career reinvention. So we all need to learn how to get better at making the most of the frequent transitions that will constitute a long working life.

There's a lot that's beneficial and necessary about this shift, but no matter how often you change careers, you're likely to experience the transition as an emotionally fraught process—one that involves confusion, loss, insecurity, and struggle. Big changes can be exhilarating, but they're also terrifying.

For more than two decades—ever since I began conducting research on the topic for my book *Working Identity*—I've been studying career reinvention: what prompts people to do it, how they go about it, and how it affects them. In this article, drawing on work I've done since the book's publication in 2004, I'll explain why such transitions are so hard for so many of us, despite their growing frequency and prevalence, and I'll offer some ideas for managing them more intentionally and successfully.

Why Change Is Hard

Some of what makes changing careers difficult will be unique to you and your particular circumstances. But you'll almost surely have to confront two challenges while in transition: a lack of institutional support and an unsettling loss of professional identity.

Lack of institutional support

Until recently, many of the important moves in our working lives were institutionalized, meaning they were well scripted by the communities and professions that oversaw them. If you wanted to become a doctor, make partner at a law firm, or move up the management ranks, you had to follow a clear sequence of steps. From schooling through retirement, you knew more or less how long each step would take. Peers went through them with you,

Idea in Brief

The Problem
Career transitions are increasingly common, yet they remain emotionally challenging. They involve confusion, loss, insecurity, and struggle. The lack of institutional support and the loss of professional identity exacerbate these difficulties.

The Solution
To manage a change in career effectively, embrace an iterative approach, experimenting with different possibilities and leveraging both old and new skills. Building relationships through bridging and bonding is crucial, as is embracing the liminal state—a period of uncertainty that allows for self-discovery and adaptation. Engaging in self-reflection and storytelling helps clarify your path and mobilize support.

The Benefits
The learning plot—a narrative of ongoing struggle and adaptation—enables you to explore new opportunities and build resilience, ultimately enhancing your capacity to thrive during and beyond a career transition.

---

and elders showed you the way. Throughout the process, gatekeepers marked your progress with degrees, credentials, promotions, and, eventually, gold watches.

Today, with the rise of nonlinear career paths, many of the transitions we make are "under-institutionalized." There is no immutable series of steps for the change you need to make, and no telling how long it will take or how to measure your progress. Complicating matters, the direction of travel is often from large organizations, which have well-structured recruiting and hiring processes, to smaller players, private firms, and entrepreneurial opportunities in unstructured job markets. Increasingly, too, people are shifting from full-time jobs to fluid, individualized portfolios of gigs and part-time roles. All this can offer you an endless sense of possibility, but it also makes it harder to figure out what you want to do, and where to start.

Loss of professional identity

Decades' worth of research in social psychology shows that our sense of identity is anchored in the well-defined groups and organizations with which we are associated and by which we are recognized. Without the cover and support of a traditional employer and a stable work identity, we can quickly start to feel lost, anxious, irrelevant, and insecure. Those feelings can be strongly amplified if instead of choosing to leave your job, you've been let go or fired.

Emotional ups and down are a standard feature of any transition. Unfortunately, you're likely to have to cope with them for longer than you might expect, for several reasons. If you're an experienced executive, you probably have some very specific skills and knowledge, and that can make finding a new fit challenging, especially because many senior positions are not advertised publicly. Vetting and interviewing processes have also gotten longer—the result of a confluence of factors, including the use of multiple screening methods such as personality tests and skills assessments. More broadly, the current economic uncertainty can make it slower and harder to secure a job or financing for an entrepreneurial venture.

Search Different

When it comes to making big life decisions, we're typically told that the first step is to figure out what it is that we *really* want. Once the hard work of self-reflection is done, the thinking goes, the rest is simply a matter of implementation.

The problem is, that approach doesn't work. Year in and year out, I've seen the same dynamic: People know what they *don't* want to do anymore, or what is no longer viable, but they don't know what to do instead. So they delay getting started, feeling that they first need greater clarity or waiting until they've lost a job and are forced to make a change.

It's easy to blame this inertia on human psychology: We fear change, lack maturity, don't understand ourselves, have failed to reflect on our true nature. But my research has led me to a different conclusion. Usually we fail to change simply because we don't know how to go about it. The problem lies in our methods, not our minds.

Career change is iterative. You can't line everything up in advance. You have to figure things out over time and make adjustments as you go.

The story of Thomas (a pseudonym) is instructive. Thomas had a conventional career in finance with a *Fortune* 500 company until he reached the age of 48. Each year he got bigger bonuses, greater performance evaluations, and bigger responsibilities, and he was eventually promoted to finance director in his company's health care business. But when that business was dismantled, he lost his job, and finding a new one proved difficult. He couldn't make a lateral move, because roles at his level were few and far between; he didn't yet have the experience to become a CEO; and he was told he was overqualified and "too well paid" for more-junior roles. Eventually he got an offer from a midsize firm that needed his expertise temporarily. It wasn't an ideal match, but he took the position to avoid having a big gap on his CV.

After that gig ended, Thomas was back to square one. But during the search process he'd reconnected with a couple of old friends and colleagues in similar straits who had pooled office space and launched freelance advisory businesses that allowed them to generate some income while searching for the next thing. Thomas collaborated with them on two startup ideas, but neither really took off, so he and his family made some adjustments: His wife ramped up her career, and they moved to a less costly city and invested in profit-generating rental properties.

During those difficult years, Thomas began thinking about a market gap he had noticed while working for his previous employer: the dearth of assisted-living facilities for the aging population in a region he knew well. Gradually he made connections with the players in that space, looked at models in other countries, and began helping companies orchestrate deals in the sector. Over time he became a go-to person for this kind of work. Now, with interest rates rising and the deal flow slowing, he's seeking an operational role again, keen to use the skills he's acquired.

What can we learn from Thomas's story? After he was forced into a career change, he didn't begin by trying to figure out who he "really" was and map out a plan before moving forward. Instead he hustled, following his nose and activating his networks, trying lots of different things, often simultaneously, without fully settling on one. He learned and adapted, which is what we all have to do in a world that rewards optionality and the exploration of many possible selves.

A Liminal State

Embracing optionality and multiplicity in the search for a new career, as Thomas did, makes a lot of sense intellectually, but emotionally it's a roller-coaster ride. That's because it puts you in what anthropologists call a *liminal state*, where you must navigate between a past that's clearly over and a future that's still uncertain.

Liminality can be unpleasant, especially for those of us used to single-mindedly pursuing clear goals on a well-trodden path. But when you're changing careers, liminality gives you the necessary time and space to question the old givens. Think of it as an identity time-out, when you can let go of your commitment to who you used to be and focus more creatively on who you might become. It takes time to discover what you want to change, identify the habits and assumptions that might be holding you back, and build sufficient skills experience and connections in a new arena. So instead of trying to land your next role as quickly as possible, you must embrace liminality. You have to be willing to get and stay lost for a while.

My research has shown that there are three important ways to make the process easier.

Diverge and delay

Finding your next role almost always takes longer than you expect. Make the most of that time. A traditional plan-and-implement program is likely only to get you more of the same. If you want your liminal period to lead to real discovery, you need to experiment with divergent possibilities while delaying commitment to any one of them. In doing so, you'll have to think more creatively and will obtain more information about yourself and your options.

Consider the case of a lawyer I'll call Sophie. Coming out of a two-decade corporate career, Sophie wasn't sure what she wanted to do next, but she was keen to explore a range of possibilities, among them documentary filmmaking, nonexecutive board roles, and sustainability consulting. Over a three-year period she got herself a board-director accreditation, took filmmaking and journalism courses, worked on a startup idea, did freelance consulting on compliance, joined a nonprofit board, did an internship in a newsroom, completed a corporate film project in her old area of ethics and integrity, and produced (and won prizes for) two short films. With deeper insight about the economic realities of the media and entertainment industries, she now feels well placed to decide between putting most of her energy into documentary filmmaking and building a more diverse portfolio of work.

Exploit and explore

Human beings are very good at either-or thinking: Either I'm leveraging my old skill set or I'm pivoting to something new. But most people making a career transition have to do both simultaneously, at least at first—ideally staying in their old jobs and careers while exploiting and exploring on the side until something new becomes viable.

One investment banker did just that when he began to tire of his career. While still working at his blue-chip firm, he started a blog lampooning the industry under the pen name Litquidity, shortened to Lit. Next, after switching to private equity, he launched the Litquidity Instagram account. As his following grew, he thought about turning his side gig into a full-time one but didn't feel he could take the risk. Reluctantly he returned to banking. But just a few years later the Litquidity business had grown enough for him to make that transition. Today Lit is a social media sensation, with several Instagram accounts, a popular newsletter, a podcast, a deal with a recruiting firm, and roles as an angel investor and venture capital scout for Bain Capital Ventures.

Bridge and bond

We grow professionally in and through our relationships with others. But when it comes to career change, the connections we already have aren't usually all that helpful. You need to build your relationships in two ways: by bridging, which involves creating or reactivating relationships beyond your current social circle, and bonding, which involves deepening ties and finding community within a close circle of kindred spirits.

Bridging often gets more attention because the golden rule of job-search networking has always been to mobilize your weak ties—the relationships you have with people you don't know well or don't see very often—to maximize your chances of learning about new opportunities. A recent study of more than 20 million LinkedIn users showed that this is indeed true: Weak ties help you get a job because they connect you to farther-flung social circles. The hitch is that most people dread the prospect of reaching out to their extended network in this way because it's hard work that can leave you feeling exposed and vulnerable.

That's why bonding relationships—critical for anyone trying to stay healthy, happy, and sane—are so important for people in transition. They provide the support, sustenance, and space people need to process the unsettling emotions of the transition period.

There's no one way to forge bonding relationships. Sometimes the important ones are with people you already know (especially spouses), but sometimes they are with kindred spirits, people also in transition, or those already working in the field to which you aspire. Thomas bonded with the buddies he shared office space with. Sophie bonded with the newsroom team (who invited her to stay on a freelance basis after her internship), a community of female documentary filmmakers, and some of the other mature students in her courses. There's convincing evidence that when independent consultants find their tribe, they are not only more productive but also better able to tolerate the anxiety of being on their own. One way or another, we all need a secure base from which to explore the unknown and turn painful feelings into sources of creativity and growth.

The Learning Plot

Being in transition is like losing the plot of your professional life. You need to diverge and delay, exploit and explore, and bridge and bond to find a new narrative thread. In doing so it's essential to engage with others and tell them your story—again and again, as much to make sense of your experience as to enlist their help. This process, which I call "self-reflecting out loud," will propel you forward, in no small measure because others will respond, sympathize, commiserate, ask questions, call your bluffs, and share their own experiences in ways that will help clarify your thinking.

Your story will most likely depart from the timeless myth in which a hero (you!) struggles to pivot to the next career and, by dint of hard work and determination, ultimately finds a happy ending. That kind of simple, linear plotline doesn't reflect the realities of today's working world, in which jobs and careers are precarious, liminality can be long, and resolution—if there is any—tends to be short-lived. So we all need to get comfortable with a new kind of narrative that revolves around what I call "the learning plot"—a story of ongoing struggle and adaptation. That's what Thomas, Sophie, and Lit all did.

As constant reinvention becomes the norm, the stories that define us have no start or ending. Instead of closure, the prize is learning: What we learn about ourselves when we embrace, rather than resist, the loss of status and identity will give us access to more options in the long term. Proficiency in being liminal won't reduce the great uncertainty before you. But it will increase your capacity to successfully navigate the present and future transitions that are the signature of a modern career.

Originally published November–December 2023. Reprint R2306L

10

Organizational Grit

by Thomas H. Lee and
Angela L. Duckworth

High achievers have extraordinary stamina. Even if they're already at the top of their game, they're always striving to improve. Even if their work requires sacrifice, they remain in love with what they do. Even when easier paths beckon, their commitment is steadfast. We call this remarkable combination of strengths "grit."

Grit predicts who will accomplish challenging goals. Research done at West Point, for example, shows that it's a better indicator of which cadets will make it through training than achievement test scores and athletic ability. Grit predicts the likelihood of graduating from high school and college and performance in stressful jobs such as sales. Grit also, we believe, propels people to the highest ranks of leadership in many demanding fields.

In health care, patients have long depended on the grit of individual doctors and nurses. But in modern medicine, providing superior care has become so complex that no lone practitioner, no matter how driven, can do it all. Today great care requires great collaboration—gritty teams of clinicians who all relentlessly push for improvement. Yet it takes more than that: Health care institutions must exhibit grit across the entire provider system.

In this article, drawing on Tom's decades of experience as a clinician and health care leader and Angela's foundational studies on grit, we've integrated psychological research at the individual level with contemporary perspectives on organizational and health care cultures. As we'll show, in the new model of grit in health care—exemplified by leading institutions like Mayo Clinic and Cleveland Clinic—passion for patient well-being and perseverance in the pursuit of that goal become social norms at the individual, team, and institutional levels. Health care, because it attracts so many elite performers and is so dependent on teamwork, is an exceptionally good place to find examples of organizational grit. But the principles outlined here can be applied in other business sectors as well.

Developing Individuals

For leaders, building a gritty culture begins with selecting and developing gritty individuals. What should organizations look for? The two critical components of grit are passion and perseverance. Passion comes from intrinsic interest in your craft and from a sense of purpose—the conviction that your work is meaningful and helps others. Perseverance takes the form of resilience in the face of adversity as well as unwavering devotion to continuous improvement.

The kind of single-minded determination that characterizes the grittiest individuals requires a clearly aligned hierarchy of goals. Consider what such a hierarchy might look like

Idea in Brief

The Problem
Health care has long depended on the passion and perseverance of individual doctors and nurses. But with the advent of modern medicine, providing superior care has become so complex that no lone caregiver, no matter how gritty, can do it all.

The Solution
Hospitals and health systems must develop grit at the individual, team, and organizational levels. That requires ensuring that all participants are committed to pursuing a shared high-level goal. Putting patients first is a common and effective objective.

How It Works
Sustaining a gritty organizational culture requires clear communication of values by leadership, programs that celebrate successes, and the promotion of a "growth mindset" that embraces continuous improvement and learning from setbacks.

---

for a cardiologist: At the bottom would be specific tasks on her short-term to-do list, such as meetings to review cases. These low-level goals are a means to an end, helping the cardiologist accomplish mid-level goals, such as coordinating patients' care with other specialists and team members. At the top would be a goal that is abstract, broad, and important—such as increasing patients' quality and length of life. This overarching goal gives meaning and direction to everything a gritty individual does. Less gritty people, in contrast, have less coherent goal hierarchies—and often, numerous conflicts among goals at every level.

It's important to note that assembling a group of gritty people does not necessarily create a gritty organization. It could instead yield a disorganized crowd of driven individuals, each pursuing

A cardiologist's goal hierarchy

In this simplified illustration, immediate, concrete goals sit at the bottom. These support broader goals at the next level, which in turn support an overarching primary goal that provides meaning and direction.

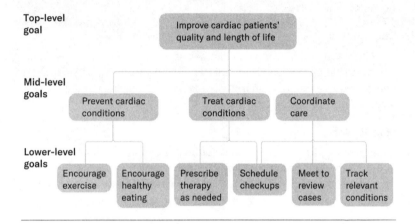

a separate passion. If everyone's goals aren't aligned, a culture won't be gritty. And, as we'll discuss in more detail later, it takes effort to achieve that alignment.

Take Mayo Clinic. It is unambivalently committed to a top-level goal of putting patients' needs above all else. It lays out that goal in its mission statement and diligently reinforces it when recruiting. Mayo observes outside job candidates for two to three days as they practice and teach, evaluating not just their skills but also their values—specifically, whether they have a patient-centric mission. Once hired, new doctors undergo a three-year evaluation period. Only after they've demonstrated the needed talent, grit, and goal alignment are they considered for permanent appointment.

How can you hire for grit? Questionnaires are useful for research and self-reflection, but because they're easy to game, we don't recommend using them as hiring tools. Instead, we recommend carefully reviewing an applicant's track record. In particular, look for multiyear commitments and objective evidence of advancement and achievement, as opposed to frequent lateral moves, such as shifts from one specialty to another. When checking references, listen for evidence that candidates have bounced back from failure in the past, demonstrated flexibility in dealing with unexpected obstacles, and sustained a habit of continuous self-improvement. Most of all, look for signs that people are driven by a purpose bigger than themselves, one that resonates with the mission of your organization.

Mayo, like many gritty organizations, develops most of its own talent. More than half the physicians hired at its main campus in Rochester, Minnesota, for example, come from its medical school or training programs. One leader there told us those programs are seen as "an eight-year job interview." When expanding to other regions, both Mayo and Cleveland Clinic prefer to transfer physicians trained within their systems rather than hire local doctors who may not fit their culture.

Creating the right environment can help organizations develop employees with grit. (The idea of cultivating passion and perseverance in adults may seem naive, but abundant research shows that character continues to evolve over a lifetime.) The optimal environment will be both demanding and supportive. People will be asked to meet high expectations, which will be clearly defined and feasible though challenging. But they'll also be offered the psychological safety and trust, plus tangible resources, that they need to take risks, make mistakes, and keep learning and growing.

At Cleveland Clinic, physicians are on one-year contracts, which are renewed—or not—on the basis of their annual professional reviews (APRs). These include a formal discussion of career goals. Before an APR, each of the clinic's 3,600 physicians completes an online assessment, reflects on his or her progress over the past year, and proposes new objectives for the year ahead. At the meetings, physicians and their supervisors agree on specific goals, such as improving communication skills or learning new techniques. The clinic then offers relevant courses or training along with the financial support and "protected time" the physicians might need to complete it. Improvement is encouraged not by performance bonuses but by giving people detailed feedback about how they're doing on a host of metrics, including efficiency at specific procedures and patient experience.

The underlying assumption is that clinicians want to improve and that the organization, and their supervisors in particular, fully backs their efforts to reach targets that may take a year or more to reach.

Building Teams

Gritty teams collectively have the same traits that gritty individuals do: a desire to work hard, learn, and improve; resilience in the face of setbacks; and a strong sense of priorities and purpose.

In health care, teams are often defined by the population they serve (say, patients with breast cancer) or the site where they work (the coronary care unit). Gritty team members may have their own professional goal hierarchies, but each will embrace the team's high-level goal—typically, a team-specific objective, such as "improve our breast cancer patients' outcomes," that in turn supports the organization's overarching goal.

Many people in health care associate commitment to a team with the loss of autonomy—a negative—but gritty people view it as an opportunity to provide better care for their patients. They see the whole as greater than the sum of its parts, recognizing that they can achieve more as a team than as individuals.

In business, teams are increasingly dispersed and virtual, but the grittiest health care teams we've seen emphasize face-to-face interaction. Members meet frequently to review cases, set targets for improvement, and track progress. In many instances the entire team discusses each new patient. These meetings reinforce the sense of shared purpose and commitment and help members get to know one another and build trust—another characteristic of effective teams.

That's an insight that many health care leaders have come to by studying the description of the legendary six-month Navy SEAL training in *Team of Teams*, by General Stanley McChrystal. As he notes, the training's purpose is "not to produce supersoldiers. It is to build superteams." He writes, "Few tasks are tackled alone . . . The formation of SEAL teams is less about preparing people to follow precise orders than it is about developing trust and the ability to adapt within a small group." Such a culture allows teams to perform at consistently high levels, even in the face of unpredictable challenges.

Commitment to a shared purpose, a focus on constant improvement, and mutual trust are all hallmarks of integrated practice units (IPUs)—the gold standard in team health care. These multidisciplinary units provide the full cycle of care for a group of patients, usually those with the same condition or closely related conditions. Because IPUs focus on well-defined segments of patients with similar needs, meaningful data can be collected on their costs and outcomes. That means that the value a unit creates can be measured, optimized, and rewarded. In other words, IPUs can gather the feedback they need to keep getting better.

UCLA's kidney transplant IPU is a prime example. Two years after the 1984 passage of the National Organ Transplant Act, which required organ transplant programs to collect and report data on outcomes such as one-year success rates, Kaiser Permanente approached UCLA about contracting for kidney transplantation. This dominant HMO would increase its referrals to UCLA if UCLA would accept a fixed price for the entire episode of care (a "bundled payment"). After taking the deal, UCLA had an imperative to deliver great outcomes (or risk public humiliation and loss of referrals) and be efficient (or risk losing money under the bundled payment contract).

The team has grown to be one of the largest in the country, and its success rates (risk-adjusted patient and graft survival) have been significantly higher than national benchmarks almost every year. With medical advances and public reporting, kidney transplantation success rates have improved across the country—but UCLA has stayed at the front of the pack.

Gritty Organizations

If gritty individuals and teams are to thrive, organizations need to develop cultures that make them, in turn, macrocosms of their best teams and people.

So organizations benefit from making their goal hierarchies explicit. If an organization declares that it has multiple missions, and can't prioritize them, it will have difficulty making good strategic choices.

Another danger is promoting a high-level objective that people won't embrace. In health care making cost cutting or growth in market share the top priority is unlikely to resonate with caregivers whose passion is improving outcomes that matter to patients.

In our experience, every gritty health care organization has a primary goal of putting patients first (see the exhibit "Aligning organizational objectives." In fact, we believe a health care organization can't be gritty if it doesn't put that goal before everything else. Though it's challenging to suggest that other needs (such as those of doctors or researchers) come second or third, if patients' needs are not foremost, decisions tend to be based on politics rather than strategy as stakeholders jockey for resources. This doesn't mean an organization can't have other goals; Mayo, for instance, also values research, education, and public health. But those things are subordinate to patient care.

Of course, even when the high-level goal is clear and appropriate, rhetoric alone won't suffice to promote it—and can even backfire. If an organization's leaders don't use the goal to make decisions, it will undermine their credibility.

Consider how Cleveland Clinic responded when it learned that a delayed appointment had caused hours of suffering for a patient with difficulty urinating. The clinic began asking everyone requesting an appointment whether he or she wanted to be seen that day. Offering that option required complex and costly changes in how things were done, but it clearly put patients' needs first. As it happened, the change was rewarded with tremendous increases in market share, but this was a happy side effect, not the main intent of the change.

As this story shows, clarity around high-level goals can be a competitive differentiator in the market and have a valuable impact within the organization as well. Data from Press Ganey demonstrates that when clinicians and other employees embrace their organization's commitment to quality and safety,

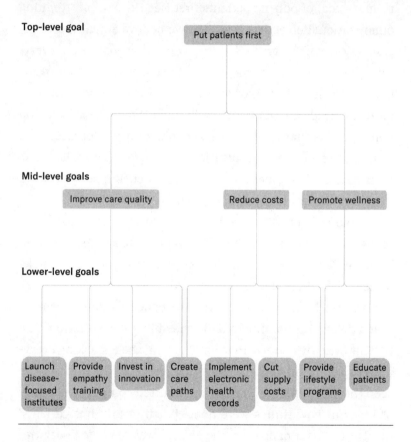

Aligning organizational objectives

Gritty health care institutions have clear goal hierarchies, like the hypothetical schematic below. As with individual and team hierarchies, lower-level goals support those at the next tier, in service of a single, overarching top-level goal or mission.

and when those goals reflect their own, it leads not only to better care but also to better business results.

But how can leaders help translate the top-level organizational goal into practical activities for teams and individuals? Seven years ago Cleveland Clinic took an important step that helped define its culture and direction. Toby Cosgrove, the CEO at the time, had all employees engage in a half-day "appreciative inquiry" program, in which personnel in various roles sat at tables of about 10 and discussed cases in which the care a patient received had made them proud. The perspectives of physicians, nurses, janitors, and administrative staff were intertwined, and the focus was on positive real-life examples that captured Cleveland Clinic at its best.

The question posed was, What made the care great in this instance, and how could Cleveland Clinic make that greatness happen every time? The cost for taking its personnel off-line for these exercises was estimated to be $11 million, but Cosgrove considers it one of the most powerful ways he helped the organization align around its mission.

Another tactic is to establish social norms that support the top-level goal. At Mayo Clinic the social norm for clinicians is to respond to pages about patients immediately. They don't finish driving to their destination; they pull off the road and call in. They don't finish writing an email or conclude a conversation, even with a patient. They excuse themselves and answer the page.

"What happens if you don't answer your beeper right away?" we asked several people at Mayo. "You won't do well here," several told us. Another joked, "The earth will open up and swallow you." A third said, "The last thing you want is to have people say, 'He's the kind of guy who doesn't answer his page.'" It's part of a bigger picture. There is more to "the Mayo Way" than a dress code (and there is a dress code). It includes answering your beeper, working in teams, and putting patients' needs first.

Another fundamental characteristic of gritty organizations is restlessness with the status quo and an unrelenting drive to improve. Fostering that restlessness in a health care organization is a real test of leadership, because health care is full of people who are well trained and work hard—but often are not receptive to hearing that change is needed. However, a goal of "preserving our greatness" is not a compelling argument for change or an attraction for gritty employees. The focus instead should be on health care's true customers, patients—not just on providing pleasant "service" but on the endless quest to meet their medical and emotional needs.

It also helps to promote inside the organization something Stanford psychologist Carol Dweck calls a "growth mindset"—a belief that abilities can be developed through hard work and feedback, and that major challenges and setbacks provide an opportunity to learn. That, of course, requires leadership to accept, and even publicly communicate, complications and errors—something that doesn't always come easily in health care. But leaders that are explicit about the need for calculated risk-taking, reducing mistakes, and continual learning tend to be the ones who actually inspire real growth in their organizations.

Crises offer special opportunities for growth—and in particular to strengthen culture. Organizations that have provided care after natural disasters or terrorist attacks have found that the experience leads to powerful bonding, a reinforced sense of purpose, the desire to excel, and a renewed commitment to organizational goals.

For example, when Hurricane Katrina hit New Orleans, in 2005, a local hospital affiliated with Ochsner Health System faced a series of incredible challenges, including power outages, flooding, overcrowding, and inadequate food and supplies. But throughout, morale remained high, because the employees all pulled together and performed duties outside their usual roles. Physicians served meals, for instance, and nurses cleaned units. "The team that was here throughout the storm has a relationship that can only be duplicated by soldiers in combat," the hospital's vice president of supply chain and support services told *Repertoire* magazine. "There's such respect and trust for one another."

Responding to self-generated crises can be a little trickier, however. But here, patient stories can be powerful drivers of improvement—especially if the stories are mortifying and involve "one of our own." At Henry Ford Health System, for example, every new employee watches a video depicting the experience of a physician in the system's intensive care unit, Rana Awdish, who nearly bled to death in the ICU in 2008 when a tumor in her liver suddenly ruptured. She was in severe shock and had a stroke; she was also seven months pregnant, and the baby did not survive.

As her conditioned worsened, Awdish heard her own colleagues say, "She's trying to die on us," and, "She's circling the drain"—things that she herself had said when working in the same ICU. Hearing her describe her experience made her colleagues realize that her doctors were focused on the problem but not on her as a human being, and that this probably was happening a lot within Henry Ford. The crisis led leadership to commit to the goal of treating every patient with empathy all the time. Today every employee at Henry Ford has seen the video, and the goal of being reliably empathic is clearly understood. Sharing Awdish's story is just one of the interventions that has occurred at Henry Ford, and during the campaign that followed the organization saw most physician-related measures of patient experience improve by five to 10 percentage points.

Gauging your grit

To see how gritty you are compared with a pool of more than 5,000 American adults, answer the questions below, tally your score, and divide by 10. Don't overthink your answers or try to guess the "right" answer. The more honestly you respond, the more accurate the results. (To take an online version of the test and get an instant score, go to angeladuckworth .com/grit-scale/.)

	Not at all like me		→		Very much like me
1. New ideas and projects sometimes distract me from previous ones.	5	4	3	2	1
2. Setbacks don't discourage me. I don't give up easily.	1	2	3	4	5
3. I often set a goal but later choose to pursue a different one.	5	4	3	2	1
4. I am a hard worker.	1	2	3	4	5
5. I have difficulty maintaining my focus on projects that take more than a few months to complete.	5	4	3	2	1
6. I finish whatever I begin.	1	2	3	4	5
7. My interests change from year to year.	5	4	3	2	1
8. I am diligent. I never give up.	1	2	3	4	5
9. I have been obsessed with a certain idea or project for a short time but later lost interest.	5	4	3	2	1
10. I have overcome setbacks to conquer an important challenge.	1	2	3	4	5

Compare your results with the percentiles below to find out if you have more or less grit than average. If you scored at least 4.5, for instance, you are grittier than 90% of test takers.

Grit score	2.5	3.0	3.3	3.5	3.8	3.9	4.1	4.3	4.5	4.7	4.9
Percentile	10%	20%	30%	40%	50%	60%	70%	80%	90%	95%	99%

The Gritty Leader

Ralph Waldo Emerson observed that organizations are the lengthened shadows of their leaders. To attract employees, build teams, and develop an organizational culture that all have grit, leaders should personify passion and perseverance—providing a visible, authoritative role model for every other person in the organization. And in their personal interactions, they too must be both demanding—keeping standards high—and supportive.

Consider Toby Cosgrove. He was a diligent student but, because he had dyslexia that was undiagnosed until his midthirties, his academic record was lackluster. Nevertheless, he set his sights on medical school, applying to 13. Just one, the University of Virginia, accepted him. In retrospect, "the dyslexia reinforced my determination and persistence," Cosgrove told us, "because I had to work more hours than anybody else to get the same result."

In 1968, Cosgrove's surgical residency was interrupted when he was drafted. He served a two-year tour as a U.S. Air Force surgeon in Vietnam. Upon his return home, he completed his residency and then joined Cleveland Clinic in 1975. "Everybody told me not to become a heart surgeon," he said. "I did it anyway." Indeed, Cosgrove performed more cardiac surgeries (about 22,000) than any of his contemporaries. He pioneered several technologies and innovations, including minimally invasive mitral valve surgery, earning more than 30 patents.

Cosgrove's development as a world-class surgeon is a case study in grit. "I was informed that I was the least talented individual in my residency. But failure is a great teacher. I worked and worked and worked at refining the craft," he told us. "I changed the way I did things over time. I used to take what I called 'innovation trips'—trips all over the world to watch other surgeons and their techniques. I'd pick things up from them and incorporate them in my practice. I was on a constant quest to find ways to do things better."

Cosgrove was named CEO of Cleveland Clinic in 2004. The passion and perseverance that made him great as a surgeon and as the head of a cardiac care team would soon be tested in his new role as leader of more than 43,000 employees. "I decided I had to become a student of leadership," Cosgrove recalls. "I had stacks of books on leadership, and every night when I came home, I would go up to my little office and read. And then I called up Harvard Business School professor Michael Porter." Porter, widely considered the father of the modern field of strategy, invited Cosgrove to visit. "He talked with me for two hours. After that, I got him to come to Cleveland. Since then, we've been sharing ideas," Cosgrove says. Porter helped him understand that as CEO he needed to be more than a renowned surgeon and an enthusiastic leader. He needed to evolve the organization's strategy, focusing on how to create value for patients and achieve competitive differentiation in the process.

Cosgrove scrutinized Cleveland Clinic's quality data, and while its mortality statistics were similar to those of other leading institutions, performance on other metrics—especially patient experience—left much to be desired. "People respected us," he says, "but they sure didn't like us." In 2009 he hired Jim Merlino, a young physician who had left the clinic unhappily after the death of his father there, and made him chief experience officer. Cosgrove asked Merlino to fix the things that had driven him away.

Cosgrove supported Merlino's many innovative ideas, including having all employees go through the appreciative inquiry exercise, and making an internal training film, an "empathy video" that is so powerful it has been watched by many outside the clinic, getting more than 4 million views on YouTube. As a result of these efforts and many others, Cleveland Clinic moved from the bottom quartile in patient experience to the top.

The institutional changes Cosgrove and his team have accomplished are too numerous to catalog, but here are a few: Swapping parking spaces so that patients, not doctors, are closest to the clinic's entrances. Moving medical records from hard copy to electronic storage. Developing standard care paths to ensure consistency and optimize the quality of care. Refusing to hire smokers and, recently, in response to the national opioid crisis, doing random drug testing of all Cleveland Clinic staff, including physicians and executives.

These changes weren't always popular when they were introduced. But when he knows he's right, Cosgrove stays the course. A placard he keeps on his desk reminds him "What can be conceived can be created."

It's hard to argue with the results achieved during his 13-year tenure as CEO. In addition to the improvements in patient experience, revenue grew from $3.7 billion in 2004 to $8.5 billion in 2016, and total annual visits increased from 2.8 million to 7.1 million. Quality on virtually every available metric has risen to the top tier of U.S. health care.

When Cosgrove gave his first big speech as CEO, he gave out 40,000 lapel buttons that said, "Patients First." We asked if some of his colleagues rolled their eyes. "Yes, a lot of them did," he said. "But I made the decision that I was going to pretend I didn't see them."

Cosgrove showed grit. And led an organization that has become his reflection.

Originally published in September–October 2018. Reprint R1805G

Discussion Guide

Are you feeling inspired by what you've read in this collection? Do you want to share the ideas in the articles or explore the insights you've gleaned with others? This discussion guide offers an opportunity to dig a little deeper, with questions to prompt personal reflection and to start conversations with your team.

You don't need to have read the book from beginning to end to use this guide. Choose the questions that apply to the articles you have read or that you feel might spark the liveliest discussion.

Reflect on key takeaways from your reading to help you adopt the ideas and techniques you want to integrate into your work as a leader. What tools can you share with your team to help everyone be their best? Becoming the leader you want to be starts with a detailed plan—and a commitment to carrying it out.

1. Many articles throughout this book emphasize the importance of resilience. What examples have you seen in your career when a team successfully bounced back from negative experiences? How do you contribute to creating a supportive and resilient work environment for your team?

2. Discuss a situation where you had to quickly shift from analyzing the causes of a problem to focusing on what you could control. How did this shift in thinking help you address aspects of the challenge more effectively?

3. Reflect on a time when you or your team faced significant uncertainty. How did you manage your fear and anxiety? What strategies did you use to navigate through it?

4. "How to Stop Worrying About What Other People Think of You" discusses the negative outcomes surrounding fear of other peoples' opinions (FOPO). Share an event when FOPO held you back professionally. How did you overcome it, and what tactics did you use to focus on your strengths, abilities, and purpose?

5. What strategies do you use to cultivate self-compassion in your daily professional life? Share any practices or exercises that you have found especially useful.

6. Consider a time when you found yourself overthinking or dwelling on negative thoughts about a work-related issue. What did you do to break the stress cycle and stay present?

7. Think of a standout resiliency program or training that you have participated in. How did it help you develop the skills needed to handle adversity and improve your performance?

8. Discuss a time when you had to decide whether to persevere or quit a project. What factors did you consider, and how did you make your decision? How might it have played out differently if you had made the alternative choice?

9. Think about a moment in your career when you felt burned out. In what ways were you aware of the three aspects—exhaustion, cynicism, and inefficacy—and how were you able to recover and regain your energy?

10. "Burnout Is About Your Workplace, Not Your People" emphasizes the importance of asking employees what they need to improve their work experience. How does your organization stay informed of how employees' feelings about work? Can you share an example of a successful initiative that resulted from employee input?

11. To counteract the pernicious effects of incivility, it is important to create a culture that rejects disrespectful behavior. How does your organization promote respect and positive behavior among employees? How do you put this into practice on your teams?

12. How do you approach addressing microaggressions—small verbal or nonverbal slights that undermine someone's values or identity—when they occur at work? Share an example of your successful intervention. How have you behaved when you realized you committed a microaggression?

13. Talk about how you differentiate between personal and professional criticism. How does this distinction help you respond better to feedback?

14. How do you handle criticism from your team or stakeholders? What practices do you implement to create an environment where constructive feedback is valued and encouraged? How do you build and maintain a network of support to help you navigate personal criticism or other challenges?

15. Consider how you balance stress and recovery in your professional life. What rituals or practices help you manage your energy and maintain high performance?

16. Discuss how a loss of professional identity, such as a layoff, has impacted someone you know during a career transition. If you have been in this position, what steps did you take to rebuild a sense of identity and purpose?

17. "Organizational Grit" emphasizes the importance of selecting and developing gritty individuals. How does your organization identify and nurture employees with passion and perseverance toward long-term goals? Can you describe a successful action?

18. How have you built and maintained mental toughness in your professional life? Share specific moments—whether you chose them or otherwise—that had an impact on your degree of mental toughness today?

19. What other sources on mental toughness have had a significant impact on your work? Were there voices or subtopics you missed in this collection? Were there voices or subtopics included that surprised you?

20. After reading and reflecting on this book and discussing it with people on your team, write down the ideas and techniques you want to try. Think of how you might experiment and implement them in both the short term and long term. Draft a plan to move forward.

Notes

Quick Read: How to Stop Dwelling on Your Stress

1. William Gerin et al., "Rumination as a Mediator of Chronic Stress Effects on Hypertension: A Causal Model," *International Journal of Hypertension*, 2012, https://pubmed.ncbi.nlm.nih.gov/22518285/.
2. Cristina Ottaviani, "Physiological Concomitants of Perseverative Cognition: A Systemic Review and Meta-Analysis," *Psychological Bulletin* 142, no. 3 (2016): 231–259, https://pubmed.ncbi.nlm.nih.gov/26689087/.
3. Jenny Taitz, "Always Waiting for the Other Shoe to Drop? Here's How to Quit Worrying," *New York Times*, August 8, 2019, https://www.nytimes.com/2019/08/08/smarter-living/always-waiting-for-the-other-shoe-to-drop-heres-how-to-quit-worrying.html.

Quick Read: Do You Know When to Quit?

1. Ryan Van Bidder, "Vontae Davis Quitting in the Middle of a Game Makes Him a Goddamn Working Class Hero," SBNation, September 17, 2018, https://www.sbnation.com/nfl/2018/9/17/17869260/vontae-davis-retired-quitting-buffalo-bills-middle-of-a-game-working-class-hero.
2. Lu Liu et al., "Hot Streaks in Artistic, Cultural, and Scientific Careers," *Nature* 559 (2018): 396–399, https://www.nature.com/articles/s41586-018-0315-8.
3. Marcus Crede, Michael C. Tynan, and Peter D. Harms, "Much Ado About Grit: A Meta-Analytic Synthesis of the Grit Literature," *Journal of Personality and Social Psychology* 113, no. 3 (2017): 492–511, https://psycnet.apa.org/record/2016-29674-001.
4. Stepan Bahnik and Marek A. Vranka, "Growth Mindset Is Not Associated with Scholastic Aptitude in a Large Sample of University Applicants," *Personality and Individual Differences* 117 (2017): 139–143, https://www.sciencedirect.com/science/article/abs/pii/S0191886917303835.
5. Torleif Halkjelsvik and Jostein Rise, "Persistence Motive in Irrational Decision to Complete a Boring Task," *Personality and Social Psychology Bulletin* 41, no. 1 (2014), https://journals.sagepub.com/doi/abs/10.1177/0146167214557008.
6. Sheena S. Iyengar, Rachael E. Wells, and Barry Schwartz, "Doing Better but Feeling Worse: Looking for the 'Best' Job Undermines Satisfaction," *Psychological Science* 17, no. 2 (2006), https://journals.sagepub.com/doi/abs/10.1111/j.1467-9280.2006.01677.x.

7. Gale M. Lucas et al., "When the Going Gets Tough: Grit Predicts Costly Perseverance," *Journal of Research in Personality* 59 (2015): 15–22, https://www.sciencedirect.com/science/article/abs/pii/S009265661530012X.

8. Thomas Astebro, Scott A. Jeffrey, and Gordon K. Adomdza, "Inventor Perseverance After Being Told to Quit: The Role of Cognitive Biases," *Journal of Behavioral Decision Making* 20, no. 3 (2007): 253–272, https://onlinelibrary.wiley.com/doi/abs/10.1002/bdm.554.

9. Carsten Wrosch, Michael F. Scheier, and Gregory E. Miller, "Goal Adjustment Capacities, Subjective Well-Being, and Physical Health," *Social and Personality Psychology Compass* 7, no. 12 (2013): 847–860, https://pmc.ncbi.nlm.nih.gov/articles/PMC4145404/.

Quick Read: Burnout Is About Your Workplace, Not Your People

1. Joel Goh, Jeffrey Pfeffer, and Stefanos A. Zenios, "The Relationship Between Workplace Stressors and Mortality and Health Costs in the United States," *Management Science* 62, no. 2, 608–628, https://pubsonline.informs.org/doi/10.1287/mnsc.2014.2115.

2. World Health Organization, "Mental Health at Work," September 2, 2024, https://www.who.int/news-room/fact-sheets/detail/mental-health-at-work.

3. Jennifer Moss, "When Passion Leads to Burnout," hbr.org, July 1, 2018, https://hbr.org/2019/07/when-passion-leads-to-burnout.

4. American Psychological Association, "Stress in America: Paying with Our Health," press release, February 4, 2015, https://www.apa.org/news/press/releases/stress/2014/stress-report.pdf.

5. Sunday Azagba and Mesbah F. Sharaf, "Psychosocial Working Conditions and the Utilization of Health Care Services," *BMC Public Health* 11, no. 642 (2011), https://bmcpublichealth.biomedcentral.com/articles/10.1186/1471-2458-11-642.

6. Emma Seppälä and Kim Cameron, "Proof That Positive Work Cultures Are More Productive," hbr.org, December 1, 2015, https://hbr.org/2015/12/proof-that-positive-work-cultures-are-more-productive.

7. American Psychological Association, "Stress in America: Paying with Our Health," February 4, 2015, https://efaidnbmnnnibpcajpcglclefindmkaj/https://www.apa.org/news/press/releases/stress/2014/stress-report.pdf.

8. Ben Wigert and Sangeeta Agrawal, "Employee Burnout, Part 1: The 5 Main Causes," Gallup, July 12, 2018, https://www.gallup.com/workplace/237059/employee-burnout-part-main-causes.aspx.

Quick Read: Recognizing and Responding to Microaggressions at Work

1. Ben C. Fletcher, "Diversity and Inclusiveness Is Good for Your Well-Being," *Psychology Today*, September 18, 2016, https://www.psychologytoday.com/us/blog/do-something-different/201609/diversity-and-inclusiveness-is-good-for-your-well-being.

About the Contributors

Amy Bernstein is the editor in chief of *Harvard Business Review* and a host of the *Women at Work* podcast.

Serena Chen is a professor of psychology and the Marian E. and Daniel E. Koshland Jr. Distinguished Chair for Innovative Teaching and Research at the University of California, Berkeley.

Angela L. Duckworth is the Rosa Lee and Egbert Chang Professor at the University of Pennsylvania and the founder and CEO of Character Lab. She is the author of *Grit: The Power of Passion and Perseverance*.

Nathan Furr is a professor of strategy at INSEAD and a coauthor of five bestselling books, including *The Upside of Uncertainty*, *The Innovator's Method*, *Leading Transformation*, *Innovation Capital*, and *Nail It Then Scale It*.

Susannah Harmon Furr is an entrepreneur based in Paris. She is a coauthor of *The Upside of Uncertainty* (Harvard Business Review Press, 2022).

Michael Gervais is one of the world's top high-performance psychologists. His clients include world record holders, Olympians, internationally acclaimed artists and musicians, MVPs from every major sport, and *Fortune* 100 CEOs. He is also the founder of Finding Mastery, a high-performance psychology consulting agency, the host of the *Finding Mastery* podcast, and the author of *The First Rule of Mastery: Stop Worrying About What People Think of You* (Harvard Business Review Press, 2023).

Herminia Ibarra is the Charles Handy Professor of Organisational Behaviour at London Business School and the author of *Act Like a Leader, Think Like a Leader*, revised edition (Harvard Business Review Press, 2023), and *Working Identity*, revised edition (Harvard Business Review Press, 2023).

Thomas H. Lee, MD, is the chief medical officer of PG Forsta, a leading provider of experience measurement, data analytics, and insights that help companies in complex industries better understand and better serve their stakeholders. He is a practicing internist and a professor (part-time) of medicine at Harvard Medical School and a professor of health policy and management at the Harvard T.H. Chan School of Public Health.

Jim Loehr is a world-renowned performance psychologist whose groundbreaking, science-based, energy management training system has achieved worldwide recognition. He has authored 16 books and coauthored the *New York Times* national bestseller *The Power of Full Engagement*. Loehr has worked with hundreds of world-class performers from the arenas of sport, business, medicine, and law enforcement, including *Fortune* 100 executives, FBI Hostage Rescue Teams, and military Special Forces.

Ruchika T. Malhotra is the author of *Inclusion on Purpose: An Intersectional Approach to Creating a Culture of Belonging at Work* and *Uncompete: Rejecting Competition to Unlock Success*. She is the founder of Candour, an inclusion strategy firm.

Joshua D. Margolis is the James Dinan and Elizabeth Miller Professor of Business Administration and the head of the organizational behavior unit at Harvard Business School.

Jennifer Moss is a workplace expert, international public speaker, and award-winning journalist and author. She is the author of *Why Are We Here?*, *The Burnout Epidemic*, and *Unlocking Happiness at Work*.

Patti Neuhold-Ravikumar is an executive coach and the former president and CEO of the University of Central Oklahoma.

Christine Porath is a professor at the University of North Carolina at Chapel Hill's Kenan-Flagler Business School and a consultant who helps leading organizations create thriving workplaces. She is the author of *Mastering Community: The Surprising Ways Coming Together Moves Us from Surviving to Thriving* and *Mastering Civility: A Manifesto for the Workplace*, and a coauthor of *The Cost of Bad Behavior*.

Tony Schwartz is the founder and CEO of The Energy Project, a consulting firm that helps individuals and organizations more skillfully manage their energy so they can thrive in a world of relentlessly rising demand and complexity. Tony is the author of six books, including *The Power of Full Engagement: Managing Energy Not Time*, which spent 28 weeks on the *New York Times* bestseller list and *The Way We're Working Isn't Working*, a *New York Times* and *Wall Street Journal* bestseller.

About the Contributors

Martin E.P. Seligman is the director of the Positive Psychology Center and the Zellerbach Family Professor of Psychology in the department of psychology, University of Pennsylvania.

André Spicer is dean and professor of organizational behavior at Bayes Business School, City, University of London.

Paul G. Stoltz is CEO of PEAK Learning, Inc., chairman of the Global Resilience Institute, and the originator of the Adversity Quotient (AQ) theory and method.

Jenny Taitz is a clinical psychologist, board certified in cognitive behavioral and dialectical behavioral therapies, and an assistant clinical professor in psychiatry at UCLA. She is the author of *Stress Resets: How to Soothe Your Body and Mind in Minutes*.

Monique Valcour is an executive coach, keynote speaker, and management professor. She helps clients create and sustain fulfilling and high-performance jobs, careers, workplaces, and lives.

Ella F. Washington is an organizational psychologist; the founder and CEO of Ellavate Solutions, a DEI strategy firm; and a professor of practice at Georgetown University's McDonough School of Business. She is the author of *The Necessary Journey: Making Real Progress on Equity and Inclusion* and *Unspoken: A Guide to Cracking the Hidden Corporate Code*.

Index

ABCD model, 59–60
Abramson, Lyn, 4
acceptance and commitment
    therapy, 50
accomplishment, 55–56
action, taking, 23–24
active constructive responding, 63
active destructive responding, 63
active listening, 99
adaptation, values-based, 144
adversity
    ABCD model of, 59–60
    bouncing back from, 1–15
    emotional traps and, 5–8
    implicit beliefs and, 8
    knowing when to quit and, 65–70
    lenses for viewing adversity and,
        2–4
    personal attacks, criticism, and,
        113–123
    questioning and, 8–13
    self-compassion and, 35–44
affective thriving, 95, 97–100
Alexander, Lorenzo, 65
Algoe, Sara, 57
alignment
    of individuals' goals, 160–164
    of organizational goals, 166–172
    team goals and, 164–166
Amabile, Teresa, 96
American Psychological Association
    (APA), 84, 85
Amirkhan, James, 4, 9
anchoring yourself, 47–48
Antonovsky, Aaron, 4
anxiety, reducing, 58
apologies, 110

Apple, 24
appreciative inquiry, 168–169
Areas of Worklife Survey, 86
Aristotle, 138
assertive communication, 62
assumptions, 78–79
attributional styles, 4
authenticity, 33, 102–103, 108
    being true to yourself and, 41–44
    leadership and, 43–44
    praise and, 62
    self-compassion and, 36–37
autonomy, 165
avoidance, 92–93
Awdish, Rana, 171

balance, 21–23
Barlow, David, 47–48
Beck, Aaron, 4
Bennis, Warren, 58–59
Bernstein, Amy, 113–123
BIFF acronym, 98–99
blame and blaming, 35
body language, 138
bonding, 155–156
Borneo, Rudy, 133–136
breadth, of adverse events, 3, 11–12
Breines, Juliana, 38, 39–40
bridging, 155–156
Brooks, David, 96
Brown, Brené, 33
Buffalo Bills, 65
bullying, 121
burnout, 71–81, 83–90
    asking better questions and,
        89–90

Index

burnout (*continued*)
  causes of, 86–87
  components of, 72–75
  defining, 83–84
  emotional and financial toll of, 84–85
  microaggressions and, 102
  motivation-hygiene theory, 87–89
  recovery and prevention of, 75–81
Burns, David, 4

Cacioppo, John, 57
Candour, 113
career transitions, 147–157
  learning and, 156–157
  as liminal state, 151–156
  searches in, 150–152
  why change is hard in, 148–150
Carroll, Pete, 30–31
Carse, James, 19
Casey, George W., Jr., 55
catastrophic thinking, 61
cause-oriented thinking, 9
Chen, Serena, 35–44
Chouinard, Yvon, 19–20
chronobiology, 135
citizenship, microaggressions on, 105
Clark, Marilyn, 131–133
class, microaggressions on, 105
Cleveland Clinic, 163–164, 167, 168–169, 173–175
Coelewij, Piet, 22–23
cognitive ability, 92, 125
cognitive defusion, 48
cognitive styles, 2
cognitive thriving, 95–97
collaborating questions, 8–13
Commor, Jim, 141–142
communication, 62–64, 99
  face-to-face, 165
  microaggressions in, 101–112
  personal attacks, criticism, and, 113–123

community, 78, 121
competencies, supportive/secondary, 126–129
Comprehensive Soldier Fitness (CSF), 55–64
  master resilience training and, 59–64
  online courses in, 56–59
  psychological fitness testing in, 56
ComPsych, 71
confrontation, 92–93, 98–99
control, 3, 9–10
  burnout and, 77
  learned helplessness and, 53–54
Cornum, Rhonda, 55
Cosgrove, Toby, 168–169, 173
courage, 117–118
courteous norms, 99
credibility, 167–168
criticism, handling, 113–123
CSF. *see* Comprehensive Soldier Fitness (CSF)
cynicism, 74

Davis, Vontae, 65
decision making, 123
  criticism about, 116–117
  cynicism and, 74
  framing and, 18–21
  by women, 123
defensiveness, 35, 122
deflation, emotional, 5–6
deliberative approach, 4–15
depersonalization, 74
dialectical behavior therapy, 50
diet and nutrition, 98, 133–136
dissatisfaction, 69
Duckworth, Angela L., 159–175
Dugas, Michel, 49
duration, of adversity, 3, 12–13
Dweck, Carol, 39, 62, 66, 170

Index

Edmondson, Amy, 122–123
Eisenhardt, Kathleen, 23
Eisenhower, Dwight D., 96
either-or thinking, 154
Ellis, Albert, 4, 59–60
Emerson, Ralph Waldo, 173
emotional hygiene, 25–26
emotional intelligence, 87, 109–111, 125
emotional traps, 5–8
emotions
    affective thriving and, 95, 97–100
    career transitions and, 150, 151–156
    emotional capacity and, 136–139
    emotional fitness and, 57
    inefficacy, 74–75
    personal attacks/criticism and, 118–119
    perspective on negative, 44
    positive, 55–56, 57, 136–137
    self-compassion and, 36–37
    sitting with, 48–49
empathy, 7–8, 57, 87, 171, 174–175
    self-compassion and, 35–44
energy management
    affective thriving and, 97–100
    ideal performance state and, 127–129
    mental capacity and, 140–143
    oscillation in, 128–129, 131–133
    physical capacity and, 130–136
engagement, 55–56, 74
exercise, 97, 132–133
exhaustion, 73–74
explanatory styles, 54–55

failure
    continuum of reactions to, 51–52
    intelligent, 122–123
    removing stigma around, 44
    self-compassion and, 35–44
family, 57

fear
    of the future, 52
    of other people's opinions (FOPO), 29–33
    priming yourself for risk and, 21–23
    reframing and, 18–21
    sitting with, 48–49
    sustaining yourself and, 25
    taking action and, 23–24
    of the unknown, 17–27
feedback, 24
    growth mindset and, 40–41
    microaggressions and, 110–111
    for your personal philosophy, 33
Feringa, Ben, 25
Finding Mastery podcast, 33
fixed mindset, 39
Fleiss, Jenny, 23
flexibility, psychological, 50
focus, 139–143
Folkman, Susan, 4
FootJoy, 141–142
FOPO (fear of other people's opinions), 29–33
framing, 18–21, 139
Fredrickson, Barbara, 57
frustration, handling, 25–26
Furr, Nathan, 17–27
Furr, Susannah Harmon, 17–27

Gable, Shelly, 62
gatekeepers, 159–160
gender, microaggressions on, 106
Gerbasi, Alexander, 99
Gervais, Michael, 29–33
gig economy, 159–160
Gillham, Jane, 54
Global Assessment Tool (GAT), 56
goals
    focus on values *vs.*, 24
    grit and, 159
    hierarchy of, 160–162

goals (*continued*)
   knowing when to quit and, 67–70
   mutual gain and, 99
   organizational, 166–172
   personal philosophy and, 30–33
   teams and, 164–166
Gottman, John, 57
Gottman, Julie, 57
gratitude, 87
grit, 65–67, 159–175
   assessing your, 172
   definition of, 159
   leadership and, 173–175
growth, 33
   post-traumatic, 52, 55, 58–59
   self-compassion and, 40–41
growth mindset, 37–41, 66, 170
   leadership and, 43–44
Gruntal & Company, 140–141

Hansson, David Heinemeier, 24
Hayes, Steven, 50
health, 15
   burnout and, 71–81, 84–85
   cognitive style and, 2
   incivility and, 92
   microaggressions and, 102
   quitting and, 69–70
health care, 159–160
helpless bystander role, 6
Henry Ford Health System, 171
hero myth, 156–157
Herzberg, Frederick, 87–88
Hey.com, 24
Hiroto Donald, 53–54
honesty, 119
humility, 119
humor, 48
Hurricane Katrina, 170–171
Huston, Therese, 123
hydration, 134
Hyman, Jenn, 23

Ibarra, Herminia, 147–157
Ideal Performance State, 126–129
identity
   loss of professional, 148, 150
   microaggressions and, 101–112
impact, of adversity, 3, 10–11
   intent *vs.*, 109
improvement, drive for, 169–171
incivility, 91–100
   holistic approach to, 94–95
   responding to, 92–93
   spirals of, 43
Inclusion on Purpose (Malhotra), 113–114
inclusive workplaces, 102–112
inefficacy, 74–75
infinite game, 19–20
integrated practice units (IPUs), 165–166
intent *vs.* impact in microaggressions, 109
International Classification of Diseases (ICD-11), 83–84, 86
IPUs. *see* integrated practice units (IPUs)

Jobs, Steve, 21
Jones, Marion, 136
journaling, 96, 144
judgment, 36–37, 42, 60–61

Kaiser Permanente, 166
Khoshaba, Deborah, 4
kindness, 36–37, 42
   incivility *vs.*, 91–100
Kramer, Steven, 96

Lazarus, Richard, 4
leaders and leadership
   burnout and, 77–78, 83–90
   gritty, 173–175

microaggressions and, 111–112
organizational goals and, 168–169
performance demands on, 129
personal attacks and, 115–116, 123
self-compassion and, 43–44
learned helplessness, 4, 53–54
learning, 33, 44
  burnout and, 78
  career transitions and, 156–157
  perseverance and, 66
Lee, Thomas H., 159–175
Leiter, Michael, 75
Lester, Paul, 64
Let My People Go Surfing (Chouinard), 19–20
LGE, 126
liminal states, 151–156
Linehan, Marsha, 50
LinkedIn, 155
listening, active, 99
Litquidity, 154
Loehr, Jim, 125–146
loss aversion, 18–21

MacArthur, Douglas, 96
Macy's West, 133–136
Maddi, Salvatore, 4, 9
Malhotra, Ruchika T., 113–123
management by wandering around, 89–90
managers
  adversity faced by, 6–8
  burnout and, 89–90
  in culture change, 63–64
  master resilience training and, 59–64
Margolis, Joshua D., 1–15
Maslach, Christina, 72–73, 75, 86, 88, 90
Maslach Burnout Inventory (MBI), 86
master resilience training (MRT), 55, 59–64

Mayo Clinic, 162–163, 167, 169
McBride, Sharon, 64
McChrystal, Stanley, 165
McNally, Richard, 58
meaning, 55–56, 78
meditation, 139–141, 144
memory, 92, 95
mental capacity, 139–143
mental health, 15
  burnout and, 71–81
  microaggressions and, 102
  optimism and, 52–64
  quitting and, 69–70
mental toughness, 59–61
mentors, 96–97
Merlino, Jim, 174–175
microaggressions, 101–112
  awareness of, 103–107
  responding to, 107–109
  what to do when you commit, 109–111
micro-pilots, 89–90
mindfulness, 98–99
Mind Sculpture (Robertson), 142
mindset, 78–79
mirror neurons, 57
Moss, Jennifer, 83–90
motivation
  authenticity and, 41–42
  growth mindset and, 38–41
  progress and, 96
  self-compassion and, 36–37
motivation-hygiene theory, 87–89
Musk, Elon, 18

National Organ Transplant Act, 166
Navy SEAL training, 165
The Necessary Journey (Washington), 103
Neff, Kristin, 36
Neuhold-Ravikumar, Patti, 113–123
Nicklaus, Jack, 142
Nietzsche, Friedrich, 55

Ochsner Health System, 170–171
opinions of others, worrying about, 29–33
opportunities, 17–18, 26–27
optimism, 42, 51–64, 87
  testing for psychological fitness and, 56
organizational grit, 159–175
  developing individuals and, 160–164
  goal hierarchies and, 166–172
  team building and, 164–166
Ott, Timothy, 23
Ouellette, Suzanne, 4, 9
overgeneralizing, 60–61

parental status, microaggressions on, 107
Pargament, Kenneth, 57–58
Parker, Andrew, 99
Parks, Rosa, 18
passive constructive responding, 63
passive destructive responding, 63
Patagonia, 19–20
Penn Resiliency Program, 54, 59
performance, 91–92, 125–146
  emotional capacity and, 136–139
  ideal state of, 126–129
  mental capacity and, 139–143
  physical capacity and, 130–136
  spiritual capacity and, 143–146
performance pyramid, 126–146
  components of, 128
PERMA, 55–56
perseverance
  downside to, 67–70
  knowing when to quit and, 65–70
perseverative cognition, 45–50
personal attacks, 113–123
personal philosophy, 30–33
perspective, 76–80
Peterson, Christopher, 4, 56
physical capacity, 125–126, 130–136

pilot projects, 89–90
Porath, Christine, 91–100
Porter, Michael, 174
positive psychology, 53, 55
positive thinking, 142–143
possibility, uncertainty and, 17–18, 26–27
post-traumatic stress disorder (PTSD), 52, 55
practice, 14–15
praise, effective, 62
presence, 46
Press Ganey, 167–168
principles, articulating life, 59
priorities, 141–142
  burnout and, 79
productivity, 84
psychological fitness, 56
psychological flexibility, 50
psychological safety, 108, 122–123, 139
purpose
  finding, job transitions and, 150–152
  personal philosophy and, 30–33
  spiritual capacity and, 143–146
  in teams, 165–166

questions
  burnout prevention and, 89–90
  collaborating, specifying, and visualizing, 8–13
  for your personal philosophy, 31–32
quitting, knowing when to, 65–70

race/ethnicity, microaggressions on, 105
reality checks, 25–26
  growth mindset and, 37–41
recovery periods, 128–129, 130–136
  emotional capacity and, 138–139
  mental capacity and, 141–142

reflection, 144, 150–152
  growth mindset and, 37–41
reflexive approach, 4–5
reframing, 18–21
Reivich, Karen, 4, 54
relationships, 55–56
  bridging and bonding, 155–156
  building strong, 62–64
  burnout and, 80–81
  energy and, 138–139
  incivility and, 99
  sustaining yourself and, 25–26
renewal, 77, 128–129
Rent the Runway, 23
Repertoire magazine, 171
repetition, 14–15
resilience, 1–15
  building, 51–64
  capacity for, 8–13
  capacity for, strengthening, 14–15
  career transitions and, 147–157
  coaching for, 7
  definition of, 2
  fear of other people's opinions and, 29–33
  fear of the unknown and, 17–27
  high performance and, 125–146
  incivility and, 91–100
  lenses for viewing adversity and, 2–4
  online courses for, 56–59
  organizational, 159–175
  self-compassion and, 35–44
  teaching, 52, 55–64
  when to quit and, 65–70
resilience regimen, 4–15
  emotional traps and, 5–8
  questioning in, 8–13
responding, styles for, 62–63
response-oriented thinking, 9
risk and risk aversion, 18–21
  priming yourself for, 21–23
rituals and habits
  balance through, 21–23
  emotional capacity and, 137–138
  incivility and, 96
  mental capacity and, 140–143
  for recovery, 130–136
  spiritual capacity and, 144–146
The Road to Character (Brooks), 96
Robertson, Ian, 142
Roosevelt, Theodore, 117
Ruby on Rails, 24
rumination, 45–50, 95
  knowing when to quit and, 69–70

safe environments, 108, 122–123
Salomon Smith Barney, 131–133
Salzberg, Sharon, 46
Schwartz, Tony, 125–146
Seelig, Tina, 22
self-appraisals, realistic, 37–41, 60
  of grit, 172
  on quitting, 68
self-awareness
  emotional capacity and, 137
  fear of others' opinions and, 30–33
  microaggressions and, 103–107
self-care, 75–76
self-compassion, 35–44
  being true to yourself and, 41–44
  fostering, 44
  growth mindset and, 37–41
  leadership and, 43–44
  self-esteem *vs.*, 38–39
self-disclosure, constructive, 58
self-esteem, 36
  self-compassion *vs.*, 38–39
self-validation, 49–50
Seligman, Martin, 4, 51–64
sexuality, microaggressions on, 106
Shatté, Andrew, 4
signature strengths, 56, 60, 61–62
Skeates, Alison, 25–26
Skeates, Jos, 25–26
Sklar, Jeffrey, 140–141

Sklar, Sherry, 143
Slavich, George, 46
sleep, 97, 133–136, 140
small steps, 23
Smith, Paul, 21
smoking, 143–144, 175
social approval, 29–33
social norms, 169
Sonos, 22–23
specifying questions, 8–13
Spicer, Andre, 65–70
spiritual capacity, 143–146
spirituality, 57–58
Stoltz, Paul G., 1–15
stories and storytelling, 58–59, 156–157
stress
  chronic *vs.* acute, 46, 129
  dwelling on, 45–50
  fear of others' opinions and, 29–33
  high performance and, 125–146
  knowing when to quit and, 69–70
  physical responses to, 45–46
  reducing exposure to, 80
  strategies for taking a break from, 46–50
success, resilience and, 5–6
Sung, Tina, 95
supercompensation, 130
supportive environments, 132
Sutton, Robert, 92
Sweeney, Patrick, 57–58

Taitz, Jenny, 45–50
Team of Teams, 165
teams, 164–166
Tedeschi, Richard, 58
thinking traps, 60–61
thriving, 94–95
time and time management, 76
  for career transitions, 153–154
  mental capacity and, 139–143

trauma, responses to, 58
turnover, 84

UCLA, 166
uncertainty
  career transitions and, 151–156
  fear of, 17–27
  sitting with, 48–49
Unified Protocol, 47–48
U.S. Army, 52, 55–64

Valcour, Monique, 71–81
values
  focus on goals *vs.*, 24
  personal philosophy and, 30–33
  spiritual capacity and, 143–146
Values in Action, 56, 60, 61–62
victimization, 6
Vistage, 81
visualization, 142–143
visualizing questions, 8–13
vocabulary test study, 40–41

Washington, Ella F., 101–112
Weiner, Bernard, 9
Wilkinson, Laura, 142–143
Woods, Earl, 142
Woods, Tiger, 142
Working Identity (Ibarra), 148
World Health Organization (WHO), 83, 84, 86
worrying, 45–50
  knowing when to quit and, 69–70
writing, 14, 96, 144

Yagan, Sam, 21–22
zero tolerance policies, 111

Zhang, Jia Wei, 38, 41–42

Work is hard. Let us help.

Engage with HBR content the way you want, on any device.

Whether you run an organization, a team, or you're trying to change the trajectory of your own career, let *Harvard Business Review* be your guide. Level up your leadership skills by subscribing to HBR.

HBR is more than just a magazine—it's access to a world of business insights through articles, videos, audio content, charts, ebooks, case studies, and more.

SUBSCRIBE TODAY
hbr.org/subscriptions